The English Country House
and its furnishings

Frontispiece 1 *Kedleston, Derbyshire. 1757–1765. A tantalising glimpse into Robert Adam's magnificent Roman-style entrance hall.*

The English Country House

and its furnishings

MICHAEL I. WILSON

CHANCELLOR
PRESS

First published in Great Britain by B.T. Batsford Limited

This edition published by Chancellor Press
59 Grosvenor Street
London W1

ISBN 0 907486 09 6

© Michael I. Wilson 1977

Printed in Hong Kong

Contents

Illustrations

Acknowledgements

The author and publishers would like to thank the following for permission to reproduce the illustrations in this book: John Bethell, nos 3, 5, 11, 14, 31, 35, 47, 50, 63, 65, 66, 80, 83, 92, 93, 95, 98; Country Life, nos 49, 58; Fine Art Engravers Ltd, nos 57, 62; Raymond Fortt, nos 67, 68, 77; E & D Gibbs, no. 69; Lawrence & Marjorie Gayton, no. 29; Noel Habgood (the late), no. 2; A. F. Kersting, nos 4, 8, 12, 18, 23, 24, 26, 32, 33, 51, 53, 55, 64, 78, 79, 84, 87, 88, 89, 90, 91; Eric de Maré, no. 17; National Monument Record, no. 36; the late Edwin Smith, nos 1, 48; Will Taylor, no. 16; the Victoria & Albert Museum, nos 19–22, 25, 27–8, 37–46, 52, 54, 56, 59–61, 71–3, 75–6, 81–2, 85–6.

Foreword

For some time now I have been lecturing to varied audiences on different aspects of the English country house. My experiences have convinced me of the need for a simple account of the architectural development and the furnishings of the country house, combined into one narrative and dealing only with essential facts. This book is the result, and I dedicate it in gratitude to all those students who have so loyally supported my lectures and courses over the past years.

2 *Compton Wynyates, Warwickshire, 1480–1520. Moated (originally), semi-fortified and secluded, but recognisably a home and not a castle*

CHAPTER ONE

From Medieval Manor to Jacobean Mansion

VISITING country houses is for many people one of today's most popular pastimes. There is nothing new about this, for the custom goes back at least as far as the late seventeenth century; the only difference is that formerly such visits were usually only permitted while the owner was away from home, whereas nowadays he is quite often present in the entrance hall to greet us, and conducts us round the house himself. In 1839 the great Duke of Wellington put up the following notice (still to be seen) at his house Stratfield Saye: 'Those desirous of seeing the interior of the house are requested to ring at the door of entrance and to express their desire. It is wished that the practice of stopping on the paved walk to look in at the windows should be discontinued.'

It is a paradox that the current very wide interest in country houses has arisen at a time when the continued existence of many of them – far too many – is threatened by financial difficulties. Such difficulties would no doubt have astonished the builders and owners of our first country houses – the Romans, whose elegant villas and gardens graced the more habitable areas of Britain for some three to four hundred years. But events nearer home forced them to contract their once mighty empire; Britain was left to her fate and then quickly engulfed by barbarian hordes whose cruder Nordic culture was totally alien to that of the Romans. The villas were either destroyed outright or abandoned, and none remains intact today. In fact, in order to get any clear idea of how they were planned and how life was lived in them, we have to go to Italy itself, and especially to Pompeii and Herculaneum. Our earliest existing country houses are therefore medieval, and moreover are of comparatively late date.

Perhaps at this stage we ought to consider what exactly is meant by 'the country house'. Generally speaking, the smaller medieval houses open to modern visitors were originally the homes of yeomen (small farmers), whilst in the larger lived the local landowners, the lords of the manor, known by the eighteenth century as squires. Larger still, both in scale and size, were the elegant country seats of the nobility and gentry, who also normally had one or more town houses. The establishment of such country seats was a late development dating from the reign of Queen Elizabeth I; before that time, out-of-town people of importance stayed either at their castles or at manor houses on their estates. Thus Elizabethan country houses such as Longleat are in a class by themselves and will be examined in more detail later in this chapter. Meanwhile the term 'manor house' is used here to include the smaller houses of yeomen, although these were not actually manor houses in the strict sense of the term.

Some readers may wonder why there are no really early medieval manor houses to be seen – very little before 1200, and nothing much between 1200 and 1400. The answer is two-fold. In the first place, the unsettled years of the earlier Middle Ages had not encouraged people of means to spend time and money on building houses except those which were defensible and fireproof, mainly castles. Even when the arrival of more basically peaceful times meant that castles became redundant, there was considerable reluctance to abandon all means of defence; this resulted in the building of some larger houses which had battlements, towers and moats, and which are known as fortified manor houses. A well-known example is Compton Wynyates (Warwickshire), where the prudent provision of such measures enabled the house to withstand for a time a Parliamentary siege during the Civil War.

Secondly, when ordinary houses of any importance were built, they were almost always of wood, though not often of oak. The long-lasting, indeed almost indestructible properties of oak have always made it the best wood for use in building, but at that time they also made it one of the most difficult to cut and shape, and therefore the most expensive. Thus during the earlier Middle Ages oak was reserved for prestige buildings only. For ordinary houses other woods were used, such as chestnut and elm, and since these do not have the endurance of oak, ancient houses in which they were mainly used have not survived.

It was not until the sixteenth century that the rise of an affluent middle class composed of a mixture of yeomen, tradesmen and the less important gentry (a number of whom gained financially by the breaking-up of the old monastic possessions as a result of the Reformation) meant that oak became available to a wider section of society who could now afford it. For these reasons most surviving medieval manor houses of oak construction date from the Tudor period, that is, from about 1500 onwards.

For many people today the most characteristic external feature of these houses is the 'half-timber' construction of black wooden beams enclosing rectangular white-plastered panels. While plenty of oak was available the spaces between the beams were small and were filled in with oaken laths, which were then covered with clay and finally coated with plaster (hence 'lath-and-plaster'). As oak became scarcer, due to the demands of the shipbuilding industry and the need for agricultural land, the spaces grew larger and were then filled in with panels of woven hazel or ash branches, which were also coated with clay and plaster; this is the 'wattle-and-daub' technique. Later Tudor craftsmen delighted to fill in the exteriors of these larger spaces with complex

3 *Little Moreton Hall, Cheshire, 1559–1589. Leaded casement windows set in half-timbering at its most elaborate and decorative*

patterns formed from shaped pieces of wood which, however, have no structural purpose. A fine though extreme example is Little Moreton Hall (Cheshire), often featured on calendars and tourist brochures.

When lath-and-plaster or wattle-and-daub infilling decayed it was sometimes replaced with brick 'nogging', in which the bricks are often laid diagonally.

Originally the oak beams were left exposed, for the medieval craftsmen knew that this would weather them to an almost stone-like hardness. Later it became customary to plaster over the beams, and much half-timbering that is seen today was in fact not intended to be seen at all. Nor was it painted black. Although it does seem that exposed timber-framing was sometimes painted in colours, it was more often left entirely unpainted, and it was not until the nineteenth century that the Victorians conceived the mistaken idea of blacking the beams. However, though historically incorrect, the decorative contrast between black beams and white plaster is certainly effective and has long been a popular feature of that modern suburban style which is neatly identified as 'stockbrokers' Tudor' (see p. 183).

It is sometimes suggested that the idea of the black/white contrast came to the Victorians via shipbuilding, having in mind such old sailing ships as Nelson's *Victory*. Certainly there is much in common between the basic structures of wooden houses and wooden ships. This is especially true of a method of timber-frame construction widely in use by Tudor times and known as 'cruck' building. The cruck itself is formed from two huge inward-curving beams joined together at the apex, rather like a horseshoe, and houses were constructed using a cruck as each end of the frame. For obvious reasons the system could be used only for cottages and smaller houses, or for portions (such as the hall) of larger houses. The final refinement was to place the ends of the cruck on a stone or brick base, rather than planting them directly into the earth where they might rot. All but the smallest of cruck buildings are formed from several adjoining sections, or bays. To see the connection with shipbuilding all we have to do is to stand our mental image of the cruck frame on its head, when the crucks joined at their apexes by a horizontal beam become the ribs of a boat, joined together by the keel.

There were, of course, stone houses, especially in certain areas where stone has always been a more readily available and therefore more traditional material than timber. But a stone-built manor house was certainly always more uncommon than a wooden one, and a surviving early example such as that at Boothby Pagnell (Lincolnshire), which dates from about 1200, is a rarity indeed. However, as timber became scarcer and its price rose, stone became more popular, until by the middle of the sixteenth century it cost no more to build in stone or brick than in wood. A keen contemporary observer of the Elizabethan scene, William Harrison, wrote in 1576 a *Description of England,* in the course of which he remarks: 'The greatest part of our building in the cities and good towns of England consisteth only of timber, for as yet few of the houses of the communalty (except here and there in the West country towns) are made of stone, although they may (in my opinion) in diverse other places be builded so good cheap of the one as of the other.' Some of the earlier manor houses offer a compromise, in that the exterior walls are of stone while those facing onto the inner courtyard are half-timbered.

The focal point in the interior planning of every medieval castle and house of any size was the hall. Originally this was practically the only apartment; in it the entire household ate together and the soldiery and retainers slept and spent their free time. A fire burned in the central hearth, its smoke wandering about before finally escaping through a hole in the roof (guarded by a small louvred turret), or through one of the small, glass-less windows, set high up in the walls in case of attack. Wooden shutters kept out the worst of the weather, for before the time of Henry VIII only the greatest in the land aspired to any kind of glazing. When it gradually became more general the individual pieces of glass were small and were joined together in a criss-cross frame formed by narrow strips of lead; the complete frame was then secured to iron bars set into the window apertures. Until 1579 glass casements were legally removable and could be left as chattels in one's will.

In the hall, dogs squabbled over bones and fragments of decaying food among the dirty rushes (changed once or perhaps twice a year) that covered the floor, which was usually of rammed earth and only occasionally of stone. In a letter of the 1520s the great scholar Erasmus gives a graphic if nauseating description of the usual state of such floors: he says they are 'commonly of clay, strewn with rushes under which lies undisturbed an ancient collection of beer, grease, fragments, bones, spittle, excrements of dogs and cats and everything that is nasty'. Meals were eaten at tables which consisted simply of long boards of oak or elm laid on rough trestles, quickly erected and as quickly removed again after use. From this comes the phrase about eating at a person's board. The lord of the manor, with his immediate family and friends, sat apart on a low dais at the upper end of the hall. Perhaps the best places at which to catch something of the flavour of medieval communal life are Penshurst Place (Kent) and Haddon Hall (Derbyshire). The importance of the hall to the medieval house is reflected in the number of times the local country house still is simply called 'the Hall'.

The dais was not the only obvious status symbol which marked the social superiority of the lord. Another was his chair. To us a chair is merely an item of ordinary everyday furniture, but this was not so in medieval times. Chairs were for important people only (hence our modern term chairman), and it is no accident that the earliest examples were more like thrones, the accent being more on dignity than comfort (though they were in fact supplied with cushions). Yet their basic construction was simple and box-like, the arms being solid and the backs high. If they have a 'churchy' appearance, this is because – in common with medieval furniture in general – their carved ornamentation derived almost totally from the arches, window tracery and other features of medieval Gothic

4   *Haddon Hall, Derbyshire. The Great Hall, with its fine open timber roof, is entered through the screen, with minstrels' gallery above*

architecture. However, it is perhaps not generally realised that much medieval furniture was also painted and gilded; a medieval man would find our modern preference for plain wooden furniture quite inexplicable.

And so, in the medieval hall, we would have found only the lord, with perhaps his lady and his chief guest, seated in chairs. The rest of the company sat on stools. The stool was in fact the universal seat of the period, and its use was continued at court (as a mark of deference to the Sovereign) long after chairs were generally accepted. A widely-used medieval type of stool was made very simply from five short planks, two forming the ends, two – or sometimes only one – joining the ends horizontally, and one forming the top. A later common type, in universal use by 1600, consisted of the square seat and four slightly splayed legs connected together almost at ground level by horizontal struts known as stretchers, which give strength and stability. This type is known as the joint or joined stool – a reference to its construction, for as with much early furniture it was pegged together with dowels of willow, not nailed (screws being a late seventeenth-century discovery), and men who made such furniture become known as joiners. The joint stool is sometimes called a coffin stool, but this is a typical Victorian misnomer; no doubt it made a useful coffin-rest when there was a death in the family, but this was incidental to its main function. In addition to the single stools there were forms and benches of similar construction which could accommodate three or more people, as well as high-backed settles, while from Renaissance Italy came the inspiration for folding X-frame stools with seats made of leather.

The medieval, Tudor and early Stuart periods – up to, in fact, the Restoration of Charles II in 1660 – are known to furniture historians as the period of oak. This is because oak was the wood predominantly used in the making of furniture throughout that long period of time. But it was by no means the only wood used; ash, elm, beech and other woods were all popular in country districts, especially those with strong local traditions in furniture-making, and the fact that hardly any early furniture made from these woods has survived in its original state only serves to emphasise the more durable properties of oak.

By the time of Queen Elizabeth there was considerable interest in giving a house a tidy, symmetrical appearance, with windows equally spaced along the house-front or façade and with the main door in its centre. Larger houses were now quite often built with two projecting wings, one at each end, giving the house the shape of an E with the middle arm missing (though this had nothing to do with the Queen herself, as used to be thought). Such symmetry, however, does not extend to interior planning. When we enter the house we do not usually find ourselves in the centre of the hall, as the exterior often leads us to expect, but at one end of a corridor known as the 'screens passage'; the hall lies at right angles to this and is entered through a door in one of the side walls of the passage, while doors in the opposite wall lead to the kitchens, pantry, buttery and so on. The hall itself may well have a minstrels' gallery from which on feast days musicians would entertain the rowdy guests below. The gallery often forms an integral part of a magnificent carved wooden screen, such screens being among the great status symbols of the age.

From early medieval times there had been a certain amount of privacy for the lord of the manor and especially the ladies of the household. Even the grimmest castles had boasted 'solars' or parlours where the lord could relax and his wife and her womenfolk could sew, chat, sing and play musical instruments. By Tudor times the principle was well established and private sitting rooms and bedrooms for the family were the norm. The servants now slept in garrets and attics, and the hall was no longer used except for communal eating (though not by the family, who now also ate apart). Gradually this practice too was abandoned, the servants having their own quarters, and the hall was then used purely for ceremonial purposes, such as a gathering of tenants or a coming-of-age celebration.

In the castle solars the cold stone walls had been hung with tapestries, as a somewhat ineffective gesture towards comfort. In the private rooms of the manor houses the same considerations prompted the much more important and successful introduction of panelling, or 'wainscotting' as it was called. This was often carved in low relief with a stylised device whose similarity to a piece of material has earned it the name of 'linen-fold'. It first appeared in this country about 1525. The panels themselves were fairly small, thin, and set in jointed wooden frames which allowed them to expand and contract, since panels which are firmly fixed tend to crack and split. Early panelling was often painted with stars, heraldic devices, the figures of saints and prophets, and so on. William Harrison comments that

> the walls of our houses on the inner sides . . . be either hanged with tapisserie, arras work, or painted cloths . . . or else they are sealed with oak of our own, or wainscot brought hither out of the east countries, whereby the rooms are not a little commended, made warm, and much more close [i.e. cosy] than they otherwise would be.

Above the panelling a decorative plaster frieze was sometimes introduced, leading the eye up to the ceiling. At the beginning of the sixteenth century a plastered ceiling was an expensive luxury reserved for the wealthiest, but by the time of Queen Elizabeth such ceilings were common. Even hall ceilings were sometimes plastered over, though more often the rafters continued to be left exposed and were sometimes carved and gilded. Ceiling decoration was carried out in moulded plasterwork giving a raised pattern which was often in the form of broad, flat bands, interlaced and geometrically arranged. This type of decoration was Flemish in origin (Antwerp being the main cultural centre of Europe in the mid-sixteenth century) and is known as strap-work. It is the most typical style of ornament used during the Elizabethan and Jacobean periods, becoming more and more elaborate with the passage of time and in its later stages also featuring (on ceilings) large pendants like stalactites. It is further enlivened on occasion with figures of animals, human portrait heads, and so on. Much of the inspiration for this strap-work came from pattern books imported from the Continent, above all those of the Flemish architect Hans Vredeman de Vries (1527–1604 or 1623).

Private rooms in the smaller houses tend themselves to be fairly small, with low ceilings, and this often combines with the dark panelling to give a rather claustrophobic effect. However, in the bedrooms this was perhaps no bad thing, for it must to some extent have helped to suggest warmth, though there was sometimes a fireplace in the main bedroom.

During the early medieval period the bed itself consisted of a fairly rough wooden frame (hidden by the bed-clothes) and a canopy or tester suspended from the ceiling; from this canopy hung a variety of costly and valuable curtains and other hangings. By Tudor times the tester (which perhaps comes from the French word *tête* meaning head) was attached to the frame either by four posts, or by a solid wooden headboard at the top end and two posts at the bottom, the latter type predominating. In contrast to the simplicity of the medieval bed, all this woodwork was heavily carved overall. The curtains hanging down from inside the tester could be pulled right round the bed, making it almost into a little room on its own – an important point at a time when privacy was rare – and also helping to keep out the cold and draughts. Holes bored along the side of the main frame had ropes threaded through them on which was supported the mattress, stuffed with rushes and wool or (in rich households) feathers and down. Here we should note that to a medieval or Tudor man 'bed' meant the mattress, the frame being the bedstead. Mattresses, especially those filled with goose feathers, were highly expensive and were specifically itemised in wills; Shakespeare's bequest to his wife of the 'second-best bed' was by no means the studied posthumous insult that most modern widows would consider it to be.

In the bedroom there would stand a chest, which could also do duty as a seat. This had evolved from the rough medieval coffer made from thick oak planks nailed together and further secured by iron bands, in which medieval households transported their valuables, linen, bed-hangings and tapestries. In those early days of uncertainty and political upheaval, not to say bloodshed, a highly portable household was essential. But as times became more peaceful it was possible to spend more money and effort on decoration and ornament for its own sake, so that among the typical pieces of Tudor furniture are the 'Nonsuch' chests, so called because they are decorated with pictures of fanciful buildings at one time thought to represent Henry VIII's long-vanished palace of Nonsuch at Ewell (Surrey). Abstract and floral designs are also common, and all these decorations are inlaid. The technique of inlaying, increasingly used during Tudor times, involved drawing a pattern onto the surface of the wood, gouging it out to the depth of about a quarter of an inch, and replacing the

5 *Jacobean bedstead incorporating the royal arms in the carved bedhead and the cup-and-cover motif in the two end-posts. (Montacute, Somerset)*

pieces thus removed with small pieces of other woods and materials (such as ivory and mother-of-pearl) already cut to shape, so as to form the pattern. Some of these woods were stained, others allowed to keep their natural colours; box, ebony and holly were especially popular.

By the time chests reached this level of elaboration their construction had also changed. The frame was now jointed and held with pegs, as in the stools of the period, while within the frame the body of the chest itself was formed by panels which were often carved with the linenfold device. Carving of earlier date – that is, before about 1525 – is usually in the Gothic architectural style, and indeed many surviving medieval chests were originally the property of churches and monasteries; however, one cannot tell this from the ornamentation which at that time was common to both ecclesiastical and secular furniture.

Occasionally other pieces of furniture are found decorated with Nonsuch inlay work. This is especially true of the small portable writing desks and boxes with sloping lids which served in the sixteenth century as bureaux; these contained small compartments and could be placed on any convenient table. A larger type of desk, free-standing and looking like a church lectern, is associated more with the earlier medieval period.

The later Elizabethan private dining room was distinguished above all by the 'fixed frame' table (as opposed to the collapsible trestle table), a weighty oblong piece made usually from oak, elm or ash, heavily carved and with four huge bulbous legs linked together by stretchers almost at floor level. The shape of these legs is usually known as 'cup-and-cover' because it resembles the ceremonial chalice-like drinking vessels which were among the chief status symbols

6 *Writing desk with 'Nonsuch' design inlaid in holly, bog oak and other stained woods. Late sixteenth century. (V. and A. Museum)*

of the period. Such legs, which reached elephantine proportions before being noticeably slimmed down after 1600, were not made from single pieces of wood but were first built up from several pieces glued together and afterwards carved to the required shape. A refinement of such tables was the introduction of the drawer-top, whereby leaves could be pulled out from underneath the main table-top at each end, thus usefully extending the length. It may be noticed that the arrival of these heavy, immovable tables effectively summarises the transition from functional, portable furniture to furniture of a more static and luxurious kind.

Also in the dining room might be found one or more forms of cupboard. To the medieval householder a cupboard was, quite simply, a board or shelf (or shelves) on which one could display cups and/or other items of family plate. What we today call a cupboard he called an aumbry – a term still used to this day for church cupboards in which sacred vessels are kept. Like the chest, the medieval aumbry at first consisted of boards nailed together, then later of framed and panelled construction, and was carved and ornamented in the usual Gothic manner. Those intended for food storage had openwork doors that were basically panels with arcading and other ornament cut through them like fretwork, so as to admit air.

The Elizabethan cupboard continued the medieval idea of a display stand, and in fact a highly popular form known as the court cupboard was much more like our modern sideboard. 'Court' here apparently has the French meaning of 'short' (i.e., low) or perhaps, by association, 'small', and the piece consisted basically of three open shelves supported in tier by four posts, the rear two usually plain but the front pair heavily carved in the cup-and-cover shape. The back between the middle and upper shelves is often filled in with a carved panel, an actual cupboard being as often built in between those same shelves. We should not overlook the importance to the Elizabethans and Jacobeans of displaying one's family plate as a status symbol. William Harrison writes: 'Certes in noblemen's houses it is not rare to see abundance of . . . silver vessels, and so much other plate as may furnish sundry cupboards to the sum oftentimes of a thousand or two thousand pounds at the least', and he then goes on to complain that the lower orders, notably 'the inferior artificers and many farmers', are apeing their betters and have 'learned also to garnish their cupboards with plate, their joined beds with tapestry and silk hangings, and their tables with carpets and fine napery' (carpets at this time being used as table coverings rather than on the floor). Much fine Tudor family plate was later melted down to pay for the alarms and excursions of the Civil War.

The rather puritanical Harrison was evidently slightly worried by the 'never-had-it-so-good' attitude of his contemporaries, though he claims to be pleased at the signs of God's apparent open-handedness. 'The furniture of our houses also exceedeth, and is grown in manner even to passing delicacy', he complains, and continues, 'here I do not speak of the nobilities and gentry only, but like-

7 *Court cupboard (also sometimes called a buffet), dated 1610, with
cup-and-cover front supports. (V. and A. Museum)*

wise of the lowest sort in most places of our south country, that have anything to take to.' Notwithstanding poverty, vagrancy and a high rate of inflation the Elizabethan age was certainly a period of greatly increased prosperity at almost all levels except the lowest (despite Harrison's remark). But in court circles the extravagance of dress, manners and language for which the Queen's courtiers were notorious was matched by some of them with an extravagance in building that resulted in the creation of some of our finest, if least typical, country houses. To these Sir John Summerson has given the name 'prodigy houses', a prodigy being something that excites wonder, and certainly nothing like them had been seen in this country before. They were symbols of new-found wealth, of rivalry (keeping up with the Leicesters, the Cecils, the Shrewsburys) and of power. It was not simply by chance that many of them were built in exposed situations where they could not fail to be seen from miles away, unlike earlier houses which for defensive reasons had always been carefully concealed. The wealth was not inexhaustible, for some of the prodigy houses were built at ruinous expense merely in order to accommodate Queen Elizabeth or her successor James I and their entourages on one of those famed progresses through the land – visits which left a trail not only of glory but often of financial disaster for the gratified hosts, even should the royal visit not last longer than a single night. Many family fortunes took decades to recover from such a visitation by the Virgin Queen. It is said that on visiting Audley End (Essex), now only half its original size but still huge, James I remarked sarcastically that while the house was certainly too large for a King it might suit a Lord Treasurer (the post held by Lord Suffolk, builder of the house).

The first of the prodigy houses to be built was Longleat (Wiltshire), finished about 1580; Summerson has called it 'the first great monument of Elizabethan architecture and perhaps, indeed, the greatest'.* It was followed by others scarcely less famous – for example Hardwick Hall, Hatfield House, Burghley House, Burton Agnes Hall. Such houses are so obviously different from anything previously built in England that the point need hardly be emphasised. However, there are a few outstanding features which they all have in common and which should be noted.

First, we can hardly fail to be impressed by the profusion and size of their windows. Glass was no longer the rarity it once had been, and although the individual panes were still small and set in lead the windows themselves had been growing larger over the years. Harrison remarks:

> Of old time our country houses instead of glass did use much lattice and that made either of wicker or fine rifts of oak in checkerwise. I read also that some of the better sort . . . did make panels of horn instead of glass. . . . But as horn in windows is now quite laid down in every place, so our lattices are also

* *Architecture in Britain, 1530 to 1830*, p. 31. 1953.

grown into less use because glass is come to be so plentiful, and within a very little so good cheap if not better than the other.

In many of the smaller manor houses from the time of Henry VIII onwards a large, two-tier bay window at the dais end of the hall had been something of a status symbol, and the oriel window (a bay supported on brackets known as corbels) was also popular. Small sections of these windows could be opened on the casement principle – that is, being hinged vertically and opening outwards. With the prodigy houses the enthusiasm for large windows became almost a mania, summed up for all time in the oft-repeated but still relevant local jingle, 'Hardwick Hall/More glass than wall.'

But these houses share another and more important common factor which the thoughtful visitor cannot fail to notice. This is the balanced and entirely regular appearance of their high and remarkably long façades, and the fact that this regularity extends to all sides of the house, so that the whole adds up to a building whose exterior is uniform and carefully proportioned. All this is so different from the haphazard medieval approach to planning that we ought to pause for a moment at this point to consider how the change came about.

In 1453 the Turks took Constantinople, and the Byzantine Empire, which had maintained something of the spirit and traditions of ancient Rome, came to an end. Many scholars fled to Italy, and their influence, combined with other factors such as the discovery of the printing press, helped to stimulate an already marked renewal of interest in the thought, art and works of classical Rome. This interest spread quickly throughout continental Western Europe and became known as the New Learning; only in the nineteenth century was our now more familiar term, the Renaissance, attached to it. Its impact on every branch of cultural life was far-reaching, and it produced artists whose names are household words today.

Basic to Renaissance architectural theory was the concept of order and balance, the mathematical proportions of buildings being worked out and related to each other so as to produce buildings harmonious both to the mind and to the eye. These ideas too the Renaissance had enthusiastically adopted from classical Rome, but it was a long time before they were adopted in England. In fact, the Renaissance made no visible impact at all on English cultural life until 1511, when the Florentine sculptor Pietro Torrigiano arrived at the invitation of Henry VIII to make the fine bronze tomb of Henry VII in Westminster Abbey. (Torrigiano had the doubtful distinction of having broken Michelangelo's nose in a quarrel.) By that time the Renaissance had already passed its peak in Italy, but England continued to stand aloof from the movement and Torrigiano and such Italian artists as may have accompanied or followed him here left no immediately obvious lasting influence behind them.

This, however, is true only of the visual arts, for it would of course be completely wrong to say that we absorbed nothing at all from the Renaissance;

on the contrary, we absorbed a great deal, more especially during the Elizabethan era. Trade, travel and the printed word ensured that we knew perfectly
well what was going on in Italy. Courtiers and gentry aped Italian manners and
dress and employed immigrant Italian craftsmen to decorate their homes;
Shakespeare's plays are full of allusions to Italian names and places, and some
are based on Italian tales.

It is therefore not surprising that the exteriors of the great new Elizabethan
prodigy houses should reflect the emphasis on balance and harmony which is
the basis of Renaissance architectural thought. But whilst in this way they reflect
the spirit of the Renaissance, as buildings their style is more French than
Italianate, and their ornamentation is overwhelmingly Flemish, the geometrical strap-work predominating. Not until 1622 was a building to rise in
London that was designed and built throughout in complete conformity with
the classical ideals of the Renaissance (see p. 35).

Those ideals, moreover, were intended to apply equally as well to the interior
planning of a house as to its exterior. They certainly played little part in the
planning of the prodigy houses, whose rooms, behind those ordered façades
and nobly-spaced windows, were seldom arranged with any great regularity;
indeed, in some cases it will be found that one window serves two different floor
levels.

In some of the prodigy houses, such as Longleat, Audley End and Burghley
House, the rooms are arranged round one or more inner courtyards in the old
medieval manner. The hall still occupied a prominent position, but it no longer
had a dais, and in some houses even its function as a ceremonial meeting place
had been usurped by the creation of an additional 'Great Chamber' on an upper
floor. The finest of such apartments is undoubtedly the High Great Chamber at
Hardwick Hall (Derbyshire) with its wonderful plaster frieze in high relief,
while the most unusual and original is that at Wollaton Hall in Nottingham-
shire. At Wollaton the windows of the hall itself (which is in the exact centre of
the house, replacing the courtyard) rise above the roof, while over it is built the
Great Chamber, creating a huge superstructure which, while perhaps not
especially beautiful, is undeniably impressive.

The increasing importance given to private family life resulted in the provision of summer and winter parlours and of 'lodgings' – two-room suites
allotted to each member of the family. These were new apartments; one which
was not, but which kept its importance as a status symbol, was the Long
Gallery, where exercise was taken, indoor games and musical instruments were
played, and where the family portraits could be hung. Normally it is to be found
on the first floor, and the prototype in this country may well have been the one
at Hampton Court, intended originally for Cardinal Wolsey's use and itself
perhaps inspired by the French Renaissance gallery at the palace of Fontainebleu.

As rooms on the upper floors began to gain status in addition to those at

8 *Wollaton Hall, Nottingham, 1580–1588. A unique prodigy house, as self-assertive as Compton Wynyates is diffident and retiring*

ground level, the staircase became something more than just a convenient method of getting from one floor to another, and became a feature of importance in its own right and often of some beauty. The stone spiral staircase (more easily defended in an attack on a castle or fortified house) gave way to a wooden one built either in a series of right-angles round an open well or on the 'dog-leg' principle, again at right-angles but without a well. The newel posts at the angles were now carved and their finials became increasingly decorative, while simple balusters were gradually replaced in popularity by flat, carved arcading. An interesting staircase of the period can be seen at Knole (Kent), in which the real arcading is copied in paint on the opposite wall in an attempt to deceive the eye. Another unusual example is the one at Hardwick – stone-built, immensely long, wide and winding, without any kind of handrail or balustrade.

Even more than the staircase, the fireplace now became a focal point for decorative treatment. Smoke no longer found its way out through a simple hole or more elaborate louvred exit in the roof. The recessed and hooded stone fireplace with wall-flue was certainly known and used as early as the twelfth century, but it remained a comparative rarity until Tudor times. Then the hood was gradually abandoned as the recess for the fire itself grew deeper; the sur-round was now often panelled and carved, while the area above the recess was given some important device such as a coat-of-arms. Bright colours and gilding

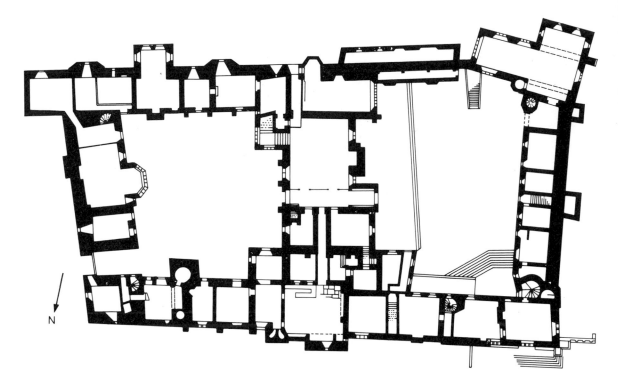

N

9   *Plan of Haddon Hall. This shows how the medieval house grew haphazardly around a series of courtyards*
10   RIGHT *Plan of Wollaton. In contrast to Haddon Hall this presents a plan of considerable regularity, the central courtyard being here replaced by the Great Hall*

were also used in these schemes, while some surrounds continued to be carved in stone. During the Jacobean period the typical Flemish strap-work decoration is imposed on fireplaces conceived architecturally in Renaissance style, the basic framework being composed of classical columns and lintels. It is noteworthy that from this period onwards the fireplace is a microcosm of the architectural styles of successive ages. As regards Jacobean fireplaces in particular, the odd mixture of Flemish decoration and Renaissance architectural detail illustrates very well the selective manner in which the English artists and craftsmen of the time took from the classical revival just as much as they felt they wanted for their purposes, though in general they were not yet fully in sympathy with the theories which lay behind it. Their chief source of Renaissance style and ornament was the highly popular seven-book treatise on architecture by the Italian architect Sebastiano Serlio (1475–1554), published between 1537 and 1575.

The smoke (increasingly acrid as coal instead of wood came into use) now escaped via tall brick chimneys whose elaborate angular shapes are amongst the most notable features of Tudor architecture. They may be seen partly as a sign

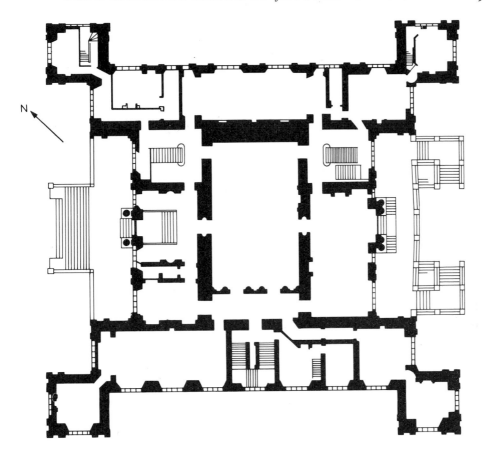

of self-assertion by the bricklayers, who at that time seem to have considered themselves somewhat neglected in favour of the stonemasons. Nevertheless, during the earlier Tudor period brick was a prestige material (as Hampton Court or even Compton Wynyates show), and its manufacture far too expensive for the majority of people to afford a whole house built of it. A chimney was the most that they could normally aspire to; this was chosen because it gave strength and stability to the house (since the chimney stack was built from the ground up as a separate entity), and also because in the event of the house catching fire and burning down totally or in part the chimney stack often survived the fire and could be used as the nucleus of rebuilding. William Harrison refers to 'the multitude of chimneys lately erected'. The black diapered patterns sometimes found in Tudor and Jacobean brickwork (and later insensitively copied in the nineteenth century) were formed from those bricks which had overheated and turned black in the kiln. During the sixteenth century brickwork seems to have been mainly confined to the Home and Eastern counties of England.

While on the subject of chimneys it is perhaps worth noting here one aspect of the prodigy houses that the average visitor rarely has the chance to see – the

11   *Montacute, Somerset, 1588–1599. An unusual view of a fine Elizabethan mansion, regular and balanced in appearance though not of prodigy dimensions*

roofscape, a huge, flat and leaded area bordered all round by a balustrade and enlivened at regular intervals by cupolas, pavilions and other architectural fantasies that from ground level also help to give these houses their unique character.

References to Jacobean as well as Elizabethan houses have been creeping into this text. In fact, as regards artistic development and progress the two historical periods are one and cannot be neatly divided by the death of Elizabeth and accession of James in 1603. Houses of the prodigy type continued to be built almost up to the outbreak of the Civil War in 1642; for example, Aston Hall (Birmingham) was completed in 1635 and hardly differs in essentials from any earlier examples, except that the hall is now clearly nothing more than an area for the reception of visitors, and as such is one of the earliest entrance halls in the modern sense.

In furniture too the progress of taste and styles continued gradually and was not suddenly interrupted by the events of 1603. Certainly more furniture was made, because houses now contained more rooms to be filled. Perhaps the most obvious changes that took place after 1603 concerned chairs. The joined armchair now became much lighter in appearance, through the abandonment of the solid wooden panels that had formerly given it such a heavy, box-like appearance; it now had four separate legs (still firmly linked at ground level by stretchers) and normal arms that rested on the front uprights and whose ends were often turned down, or 'scrolled'. Even more importantly, however, there appeared for the first time the armless chair, known originally as a back-stool. In fact it was much like a broader version of the joint stool with two of the legs continued upwards so as to form uprights, to which a padded back was attached; the seats too were padded, and a favourite covering was 'turkey-work', in imitation of imported Middle Eastern carpets. Silks and velvets were also favoured for upholstery, but there was not much of this on any form of seat furniture before 1660.

Chairs and stools on the X-frame principle continued to be made; these too were padded, as was also a version of the backstool with arms, a much broader

12 *Hatfield House, Hertfordshire, 1607–1611. The Long Gallery, complete with panelling, ornate plaster ceiling (originally white) and two impressive and typical Jacobean fireplaces*

and wider affair than the backstool proper. During the nineteenth century the latter became known as a 'farthingale chair', in the belief that it had been developed in order to accommodate the large hooped skirts worn by women of the period. There is nothing either to prove or disprove this theory.

Some further concession to comfort was made in the form of the day-bed, forerunner of the couch, on which one could take an afternoon nap. This was simply a low, solid wooden bedstead with sloping headboard, and was softened by the addition of a loose mattress or cushions. More luxurious was the famous 'Knole' settee, so called because the earliest known example forms part of the valuable collection of early seventeenth-century furniture at Knole. It consists of a velvet-upholstered settee with a back and two sides which can be let down, so that the whole converts into a form of day-bed. However, there seems to be some doubt as to its exact date, some experts stating that it can be no earlier than about 1640.

Generally speaking, the carved decoration of Jacobean solid wood furniture becomes deeper and more extravagant than it had been during the sixteenth century. This is especially true of larger items such as beds and court cupboards, where it seems almost to be inspired by a kind of frenzy, a grim determination to leave no visible wooden surface free from the mixture of Flemish strapwork and Renaissance ornament, some of it very grotesque. It is only fair to say that this impression is conveyed by Jacobean ornament in general, not just that applied to furniture. Yet in other respects there was a welcome move towards greater simplicity; for example, the grossly bulbous legs of the heavy draw-leaf tables tended, after 1600, to decrease in girth until in some late examples they are no more than plain columns, the cup-and-cover outline being completely abandoned. (A notable Jacobean motif was the obelisk, a symbol of prestige and power, seen perhaps at its most obvious on the tombs of the period.)

The columnar supports of chairs, tables and the like, carved with raised and incised rings, were produced by the technique of turning. In essence, the leg or other member to be shaped was attached to a spinning device which in those days consisted of a horizontal springy pole at the top (in the country, where the work was often done out of doors or under a simple shelter, the branch of an actual sapling would be utilised) and a pedal at the bottom, both united by a rope. By maintaining tension between these two points the turner kept the wood spinning round and shaped it with chisels as it spun. Although in country districts the craftsman was usually jack-of-all-trades, in the cities the demarcations between turning, carving and joining were rigidly observed, there being separate exponents of each separate trade.

Very many variations of turning were possible. One which became especially popular during the Jacobean period was bobbin-turning, resembling a series of balls strung together. Sometimes whole chairs were decorated in this manner, and the effect then becomes monotonous, if not positively ugly. In fact ugliness and extravagance are undeniably the keynotes of much architecture, decoration and furniture as the Golden Age of Elizabeth merged into the more vulgarly opulent one of James, and as this in turn hovered on the brink of those increasingly turbulent years that were destined to end in the fratricidal bloodshed of 1642.

13 *Jacobean backstool ('farthingale chair'). Sturdy stretchers joining the legs at floor level give greater strength and stability. (V. and A. Museum)*

CHAPTER TWO

Restoration Grandeur

IN ORDER to understand the further development of the country house we must spend a little more time in discussion of Renaissance influence. As we have already noted, a basic essential of Renaissance architectural theory was the concept of order and balance, the proportions of buildings being mathematically worked out and related to each other. These ideas were not new. In fact they stemmed from classical Roman theories on architecture, many of which had been written down in the 1st century AD by a military engineer named Vitruvius. His manuscript was lost for centuries until it was rediscovered and published at Rome in about 1486, other editions following in 1511, 1521, 1545 and 1556. The work engendered tremendous excitement, as the number of editions shows, and may be said to have brought about a revolution in architectural thinking at a time when the mind of Renaissance man was open and fully receptive to new and challenging ideas. Moreover the influence of Vitruvius was not only deep but also long-lasting, as we shall see.

One of the most important Italian architects to absorb the full measure of the Vitruvian style was Andrea Palladio (1508–1580), who lived and worked mainly in Vicenza. In 1570 he too produced a highly influential work on the theory and practice of architecture, *I Quattro Libri dell' Architettura* (The Four Books of Architecture). The name of Palladio was to have especial significance in the story of the English country house.

Yet although Vitruvius was known and read in sixteenth- and early seventeenth-century England, * classical theories of architecture were not fully appreciated or understood there, while the classical style was imitated only in superficialities, as the prodigy houses show. Except, that is, in the work of one man, the great Inigo Jones (1573–1652). In 1615 Jones (originally a painter and designer of scenery and effects for court entertainments) was appointed Surveyor of the King's Works, an important administrative post which also

---

* 'Our principal master is Vitruvius' (Sir Henry Wootton, *The Elements of Architecture*, 1624). Almost 50 years earlier William Harrison had written: 'If ever curious building did flourish in England, it is in these our years, wherein our workmen excel, and are in manner comparable in skill with old Vitruvius . . .' (1577).

entailed architectural work. He had already visited Italy twice, and while there had been able to study at first hand the work of the Renaissance architects as well as existing classical Roman remains. As a result he became imbued with a genuine feeling for classicism, the only English architect of his age fully to grasp the principles of Italian Renaissance building and to put them into practice. His especial interest in Palladio is shown by his own carefully annotated copy of *I Quattro Libri* which is still preserved today in the library of an Oxford college (Worcester), though it is only fair to say that other Italian architects of the period also helped to influence his style.

Jones's most complete expression of the new Italian manner is the famous Banqueting House in London's Whitehall, the first building in England to show the full impact of the Renaissance. Many people today pass it by without a second glance, either because they are too familiar with it, or because it is swallowed up anonymously in the great mass of buildings around it. When completed in 1622, however, it stood out high and proudly from the jungle of old wooden medieval and Tudor buildings which then formed the royal palace of Whitehall. The Banqueting House was to be the nucleus of a fine new palace, but this was never built, and the old palace was finally destroyed in 1698 in a fire which only the Banqueting House itself happily survived.

Its carefully balanced proportions and style of decoration mark out the exterior of the Banqueting House as thoroughly Italianate in conception and totally different from any previous English building. It is as though one of Palladio's palaces at Vicenza had been snatched up by some giant hand and set down again in the centre of London. One gets a similar impression from another of Jones's works, the Queen's House at Greenwich, an out-of-town residence originally intended for James I's wife Anne of Denmark but finally completed in 1635 for Queen Henrietta Maria. This is England's first domestic building designed in almost all respects according to classical theories, as opposed to a semi-public building like the Banqueting House. Moreover the latter contains only a single large main apartment, although the proportions of that room, with its magnificent ceiling paintings by Rubens, are totally harmonious. In the Queen's House the planning of all the rooms, both individually and as related to each other, is likewise based on careful mathematical calculations; for example, the hall, which rises through both main floors, is in fact a 40-foot cube, a feature which was to be repeated in more than one country house as yet unbuilt.

Cubic proportions seem to have fascinated Jones, who constantly based his plans on them (though the cube was too obvious and useful a spatial module to be ignored by anyone building in the classical style). The best-known example of this is his famous Double Cube Room at Wilton House (Wiltshire) which, with the Single Cube Room next door exactly half its size, is a classic example of the system of 'harmonic proportions', as it was called. The room as it now stands is a reconstruction of the late 1640s by Jones's pupil, assistant and kins-

14   *The Queen's House, Greenwich. By Inigo Jones, 1611–1635. An Italianate villa on the fringes of London*
15   RIGHT *Plan of the Queen's House, exemplifying the 'harmonic proportions' of Italian Renaissance classicism*

man John Webb, but there is no reason to suppose that the proportions differ in any way from the original.

The south front of Wilton, which includes the Double Cube Room and is usually associated with the name of Jones, was probably actually built by another architect named Isaac de Caus in the 1630s. However, Jones seems to have recommended de Caus as he was too busy to undertake the work himself, and certainly it was created in consultation with him. The façade of the south front presents us, even more obviously than does the exterior of the Queen's House, with Italian ideals of balance and symmetry which are here far more authentic than on the rather frenzied and over-ornamented façades of the prodigy houses. The details too are purely Italian, not Flemish, and include the ornamental window-shades and the great central window of a type often called either 'Palladian' or 'Venetian', distinguished by a central arched section flanked by two shorter, flat-headed sections.

Yet as it happened, the classical precepts which meant so much to Jones were not to be the governing factor in building either publicly or privately for almost a century to come. The nation was not yet ready for classical-style architecture as perfected by Palladio and interpreted by Jones and his few

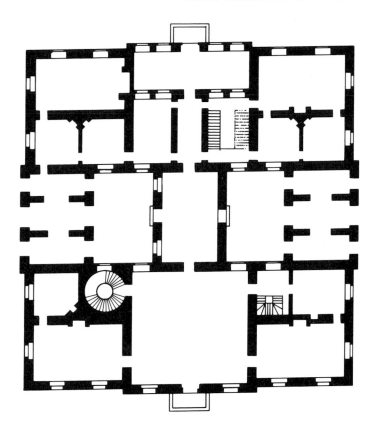

immediate followers. What is more, it had far more serious matters on its hands in the shape of the Civil War which broke out in earnest in 1642. Not until the dust of that conflict had settled was there time or money for building, and even then the austerities of the Commonwealth ensured that only a handful of great houses were built during that period.

One, however, was outstanding. Coleshill in Berkshire was begun about 1650 by Roger Pratt (1620–1685), a gentleman amateur who built only five houses altogether, though this small number is quite outweighed by their importance. Until the 1920s it was generally assumed that Inigo Jones was the architect of Coleshill, and indeed we know that Jones knew Pratt and visited the house with him. But there is now no doubt that it was in fact the work of Pratt, though Jones may have offered advice. Obviously Pratt was familiar with the work of Jones, but he had also spent several years on the Continent, from 1643 to 1649, during which he travelled through France, Italy and the Netherlands absorbing the different architectural styles of those countries, above all that of Palladio. But Pratt was sufficiently a genius in his own right to be able to create a style recognisably his own, and one that was to prove of great influence. In passing it ought perhaps to be stressed here that although the

16   *Wilton House, Wiltshire. The Italianate south front (of the 1630s) is usually associated with Inigo Jones though not actually built by him*

17   *Coleshill, Berkshire. Built in the 1650s by Roger Pratt, it epitomised most of the chief external features of the later seventeenth-century country house*

term 'architect' itself was freely used, there was really no such thing as a professional architect in the modern sense, complete with an office and pupils, until the nineteenth century. Most country houses were built by the owners, many of whom would be well read in the accepted theories of architecture, in consultation with local master builders and master carpenters and often using plans and ideas culled from printed pattern books.

Coleshill was the most satisfactory summary to date of most of the essential external features that were to distinguish the average country house of the second part of the seventeenth century. Amongst these were a flat-topped, steeply-pitched roof with attic or dormer windows, very tall chimney stacks, a high proportion of regularly spaced windows, a lantern or cupola in the centre of the roof, and a stone or wooden balustrade running round the roof-ridge.

Sad to say, we cannot visit Coleshill today, for it was burnt out in a fire in 1952 and the shell demolished. Nor can we visit Pratt's second most influential house, for although built after the Restoration during the years 1664 to 1667 it too was demolished as early as 1683. This was Clarendon House in London's Piccadilly (then little more than a country lane), built for Charles II's powerful but later discredited Chancellor, Lord Clarendon. But in addition to the features already introduced at Coleshill, Clarendon House had two forward-projecting wings and a projecting central block in the façade surmounted by a triangular gable-end known in architecture as a pediment.

Pratt was knighted in 1668 and retired into rural obscurity in his native Norfolk. But the combined influence of Coleshill and Clarendon House was felt right through into the eighteenth century, and a large number of Pratt-type country houses were built, most of which reflect more or less adequately Pratt's success at Coleshill in combining Italian, Dutch, French and English ideas into one cohesive and brilliant whole.

Another highly influential type of house – plainer, squarish, built of brick with stone enrichments – was primarily of Dutch origin, and was promoted in this country after the Restoration by Hugh May (1622–1684), an architect who had spent most of the Commonwealth period in Holland as a member of the Duke of Buckingham's household and later received a royal appointment from Charles II. Frequently a house of the period may reflect the combined influence of Pratt and May, and it is they, not Sir Christopher Wren (1632–1723), who we must thank for establishing what is often mistakenly called the Wren type of house. Wren himself was primarily a builder of palaces, churches, and other large public works, not country houses. He can be credited with only a conjectured handful of these (Winslow, Buckinghamshire, is a possibility), and all were built long after the type had been firmly established. We do not, therefore, look to Wren as a country house architect, and in the absence of documentary evidence we should regard with suspicion any claims for his authorship that may be put forward in connection with specific houses.

The interest in Dutch architecture at this time also helped to bring about the renewed general popularity of brick as a suitable building material on its own, not just for decoration or the construction of chimneys. At the same period (about 1660) the method of laying bricks, called 'bonding', also changed; 'English bond', in which rows of bricks all showing their sides alternated with rows showing their ends, was replaced by 'Flemish bond', in which sides ('stretchers') and ends ('headers') alternate throughout each row. With this difference in mind it is therefore possible to hazard a guess as to the approximate date of an old brick-built house or free-standing wall. The second half of the seventeenth century is our finest period of brick building, the bricks themselves being a wonderfully rich red colour.

Windows too came under Dutch influence, for the sash window which had long been popular in Holland now arrived to replace the old-fashioned casement, and was found in all but the smallest houses by the end of the seventeenth century. No greater act of vandalism in altering an old house can be perpetrated than by replacing such windows with modern plate glass and removing the glazing bars (the criss-cross wooden struts which frame the glass panes); somehow this seems to convert the house instantly from a living entity to a dead, soulless thing, the modernised windows looking like the blank eyes of a sightless person.

Almost all the houses in the new style naturally date from after 1660, the date of Charles II's Restoration after the final collapse of the Commonwealth. Not until then did men have the time, money or confidence to devote to building houses. After 1660, however, there was a very great increase in building activity all over the country. 'This day the month ends . . . and all the world in a merry mood because of the King's coming', wrote Samuel Pepys in his famous diary on 31 May 1660, Charles having landed at Dover just a week previously. The sense of a new beginning and a fresh start was soon expressed just as much in furniture as in architecture or social life. What is more, the King and his court brought back from their long Continental exile a taste for new ideas, new designs, and above all the luxury and fashions then in vogue at Versailles, which set the tone for all the other European courts. After the years of Cromwellian austerity the nation was more than ready to follow the court's lead and to adopt those ideas with enthusiasm, with the result that a complete and marked change becomes immediately apparent in the furniture of the time. Oak became old-fashioned almost overnight, it seemed, and was replaced as the fashionable wood by walnut (though walnut was already in use long before the Commonwealth era: for example, walnut furniture was made in 1587 for Wollaton Hall).

The immediate popularity of walnut is soon explained. It was more elegant, capable of much finer cutting than oak, its colour richer and its grain more exciting. Its fashionable *cachet* is perhaps nowhere better illustrated than at Ham House (Surrey), where in the 1670s extensive use was made of deal panelling painted and grained to look like walnut in a deliberate attempt to impress the

18 *Eltham Lodge, Kent. By Hugh May, 1663–1664. The pediment and stone pilasters were adopted as important features of many a post-Restoration house*

visitor, though of course at considerably lower cost. Native supplies of walnut were not nearly sufficient to satisfy demand, and much was imported from France, Spain and Virginia. In his book *Sylvia, or a Discourse of Forest Trees* (1670), the diarist John Evelyn makes an interesting comment on this scarcity, as well as on efforts to imitate the grain and colouring of walnut:

> In truth, were this timber [walnut] in greater plenty amongst us, we should have far better utensils of all sorts for our houses, as chairs, stools, bedsteads, tables, wainscot, cabinets &c. instead of the more vulgar Beech, subject to the worm, weak and unsightly; but which, to counterfeit and deceive the unwary, they wash over with a decoction made of the green husks of Walnuts &c.

(Evelyn had evidently not yet discovered the weaknesses of walnut itself.) At the same time it is worth remembering that country craftsmen have always been less influenced by fashionable trends than their urban counterparts, so that after 1660, outside London and a few other main towns, furniture on traditional Jacobean and early Stuart lines continued to be made in oak and other woods until well on into the eighteenth century.

There now appeared walnut chairs with long, narrow backs formed of oblong or oval panels of woven cane between turned uprights, the seats too being often also of cane. This use of cane was another innovation, and had the effect of making the chairs seem much lighter in their general appearance,

19 *Walnut chair with seat and back panel of cane, about 1660. The rather crudely-carved cherubs-and-crown motif in the back is repeated in the front stretcher. (V. and A. Museum)*

20 *Walnut-and-beech chair with seat and back of cane, later seventeenth century. The arched cresting rail and front stretcher point to Dutch influence. (V. and A. Museum)* though in fact they continued to be quite heavily carved in places, especially on the stretcher between the front legs. A favourite motif for this carving was two cherubs holding between them a crown, usually repeated in the crest of the chair-back. (But though a usefully patriotic reference to the Restoration, the motif was known and used on the Continent and indeed even in England before 1660.) The use of cane in seats and backs continued until the 1740s, though it was supposedly unfashionable by the 1690s. A type of scrolled foot of Spanish origin and known as the 'Braganza' foot was introduced as, it is said, a compliment to Charles II's Portuguese Queen Catharine of Braganza.

As the century wore on chairs in general became taller and narrower, their crests and front stretchers usually arched and the seats low, and some very curiously-shaped 'housemaid's knee' front legs appeared, having a pronounced and sharp bump at the knee. Many chairs of this type were made of beech, 'ebonised' – painted black to look like ebony. In these and much other furniture of the time there is Dutch-cum-French influence that first began at the Restoration, grew stronger in the 1680s and was later even more strongly reinforced by the influence of a French-born designer named Daniel Marot (1663–1752), who from 1694 to 1698 was employed in this country by William III as an advisor on artistic matters. In this capacity Marot was consulted on a wide range of topics including interior decoration and planning, furniture, and garden layout.

Chairs were now made in sets, often with matching stools, and no distinction was made between those intended for saloons and those for dining rooms. With the Restoration the custom of eating meals in rooms specially set apart for the purpose became firmly and universally established, and the Jacobean fixed-frame table was replaced in popularity by the familiar oval or round (occasionally square or rectangular) gate-legged table, consisting of a solid central frame of four legs and with flaps at each long side supported by an extra swing-leg or, more rarely, a pair of the same. The gate-legged table had in fact been coming into popular favour some time before 1660; perhaps partly because of this, partly because of the need for greater strength and stability, it continued to be made of oak, yew or elm.

Although some large gate-legged tables could accommodate quite a number of people, it was now fashionable to dine in the French manner – that is, with the company seated round several smaller tables instead of at a single large one. In 1679 the Great Eating Room at Ham House contained 8 small tables and 18 chairs; however, there was also a private dining room in which the family normally ate. Kitchens were often on the ground floor, but it was during the seventeenth century that the basement or semi-basement kitchen first appears. Having visited Eltham Lodge (architect, Hugh May) whilst it was being built in 1664, the diarist John Evelyn complains that the house is 'not well contrived; especially the roof and rooms too low pitched, and the kitchen where the cellars should be.' Yet Pratt had already established the type at Coleshill,

21 *Page of designs by Daniel Marot for chairs, matching stools, and window curtains with valances. Curtains were frequently draped in this theatrical manner throughout the later seventeenth and the eighteenth centuries*

22   *Side table veneered in walnut with floral marquetry, later seventeenth century. The shallow drawer, fine twist-turned legs and H-shaped stretcher are all typical. (V. and A. Museum)*

and gives cogent reasons for doing so: 'It will be convenient . . . that all the rooms be so ordered that they may be most of service, but not in the least kind of incumbrance to each other, viz: the kitchen and all its offices to lie together, and the buttery and cellar with theirs, etc. and all these to be disposed of in a half ground storey, with their backcourts, convenient to them; in that no dirty servants may be seen passing to and fro by those who are above, no noises heard, nor ill scents smelt.'*

The main decorative interest of gate-legged tables is in the turning of the legs, which may take many different forms. The art of the turner was considerably advanced after 1660 by the perfection of the 'barley sugar' twist, a beautiful spiral form used for the stretchers and back uprights of chairs, but even more so for the legs of the various small occasional tables which now began to appear. These tables are usually square or oblong; those which are finished on all four sides were intended to stand in the centre of a room, but those finished on three

* This and the following quotations are taken from Pratt's notebooks as edited by R. T. Gunther under the title *The Architecture of Sir Roger Pratt*, 1928.

sides only are 'side' tables, to be placed against a wall. Some were entirely ornamental, not functional, their surfaces covered with raised designs in gesso, a type of paste which was built up in several coats and then, having set hard, was carved and gilded. Such tables often formed part of a curious ornamental grouping which also included a hanging mirror and two large freestanding candlesticks.

Ostentation such as this was matched by the magnificence of the apartments in which it was displayed. Plaster ceilings were still in vogue, but the shallow and overall strapwork designs of an earlier age now gave place to a grid-like pattern of heavy beams with deeply-carved plaster mouldings surrounding a great round or oval centrepiece. (Pratt says that the divisions of the ceiling ought to be nine in number, and to be as large as practicable.) While the design of this type of ceiling derives yet again from classical Roman sources (and had been used by Inigo Jones at the Banqueting House and the Queen's House, for example), as do many of the plasterwork motifs used in it, other motifs are in a naturalistic style often executed in very high relief (Pratt mentions 'fruits, flowers, leaves of oak, laurel trails etc'.). With the ceiling often went a plaster frieze; Pratt's pleasant suggestions for this are that it should be 'filled with a running work of some noble leaf and flower of which many designs are to be had, or with what will be yet more delightful, festoons ingeniously contrived either of fruit, flowers, or both together and between each of them either a little boy laughing, playing, or in some other pretty action, or an escutchion with the arms of the patron etc'. Some of the finest plasterwork of the period in this country may be seen at Sudbury Hall (Derbyshire), completed during the years 1670 to 1695 by two craftsmen named Bradbury and Pettifer.

The naturalistic style is closely associated with the wood carvings of the great Grinling Gibbons (1648–1717). The later seventeenth century is marked by the fact that first-class craftsmen who formerly would have been employed only by the Crown now also worked for private patrons. Gibbons is the best known of such craftsmen, and probably the greatest in his chosen medium, though he also worked in stone and bronze. Born in Rotterdam of English parents, he was working in this country by about 1670 and was brought to the notice of Charles II by John Evelyn; he subsequently held the post of Master Carver to the Crown until 1714, but this did not prevent him from accepting many private commissions. However, as with beds slept in by Queen Elizabeth I and houses built by Wren, we need to be careful in assigning work to Gibbons, for he was only the first among a number of important carvers active at that time but whose names are not generally known. Nevertheless, authentic work by Gibbons abounds, and particularly good examples may be seen at Petworth (Sussex) and Belton House (Lincolnshire). His favourite wood was lime, but there is no truth in the old story that he used a carved pea-pod as a kind of signature, for in fact most other carvers of the period also used this motif.

Whether by Gibbons or not, the panelled walls of many a room of the period

23   *Sudbury Hall, Derbyshire. The Long Gallery (now minus bookcases) boasts one of*
the finest plaster ceilings of the whole Restoration period.

24   *Detail of a carved wooden trophy of fish, fruit and game from the chimneypiece of the Drawing Room at Sudbury Hall. The complete chimneypiece is an early authentic work by Grinling Gibbons and was carved in 1678 for the sum of £40.*

are enlivened by great swags and cascades of flowers, fruit, dead game, weapons, musical instruments and other items, all carved from wood. The panels themselves were now much larger and were of oak, fir or cedar, occasionally walnut. They served as a neutral background for the pictures which were now becoming popular, especially portraits; such paintings were either set into the panelling or else were placed in elaborately carved frames and suspended on chains which were swathed in lengths of coloured silks. Paintings were also incorporated into fireplace surrounds and doorways, 'over each of which if some little picture, but chiefly some pleasant landscape of ruins and trees be put, it will add much grace to the place where they are', remarks Pratt. Fireplaces were now of marble and followed purely architectural lines first established by Inigo Jones; the most characteristic feature is a square frame above the mantelpiece surmounted by a pediment.

However, painting at this period was no longer necessarily confined within frames. Entire ceilings, and sometimes walls as well, were covered with scenes and simulated architecture by artists who specialised in such work. The scenes are usually concerned with the activities of the various classical gods, and in England three artists in particular were celebrated for this type of painting; they were the Neapolitan Antonio Verrio (1639–1707), the Frenchman Louis Laguerre (1663–1721: both of these made their homes here), and Sir James Thornhill (1675–1734). Examples of their work may be seen in country houses both large and small, all over England, but Verrio's most famous work is at Burghley House, where he painted a whole suite of state rooms, Laguerre's the Saloon at Blenheim Palace, and Thornhill's the great Painted Hall of Greenwich Hospital. The chief feature of all their mural decoration is the skill with which they use the age-old devices of perspective and illusionism or *trompe l'œil*, so as to make it difficult for the onlooker to decide immediately where ceiling ends and walls begin, what is sculpture or stonework and what paint, what is real and what is false. (However, Roger Pratt seems not to have been so easily taken in, for he writes:

> But as for those [figures] which are ascending, or sitting as it were there, they cannot but be represented to us with much shortening and distortion, and so have something of harsh and monstrous in them, though performed by the most experienced masters in that curious art of perspective, as will most evidently appear to all men upon the least observation.)

Tapestry continued to be used as wall-covering, but flock wallpaper, mounted on stretchers, also became popular at this time, whilst at Ham House the walls of the private dining room are covered in stamped and gilded leather. In addition to the imitation walnut panelling at Ham, in other rooms there the deal boards are painted and grained to look like marble. This may partly be seen as one aspect of the contemporary interest in illusionism, of which the mural decoration of Verrio and Thornhill is a larger expression. At the same

25 *Ham House, Surrey. From the White Closet, with inset pictures over the door and fireplace, imitation marble panelling, and ceiling painted by Verrio, we get an uninterrupted view through a typical string of connected state rooms*

time it should be emphasised that during the seventeenth century the painting, graining or marbling of panelling and other woodwork was the rule rather than the exception to it.

A notable feature of rooms in general is the increased height of ceilings. As a result of this beds became taller and more imposing; at the same time the posts became more slender, and there was a tendency to hide as much as possible of the posts and frame beneath rich upholstery and drapery. Often an elaborate headboard was carved from pinewood and then covered with material. The four corners of the tester itself were crowned with decorative urns or other finials, and persons of rank were entitled to plumes of highly-prized ostrich feathers as well. Today these plumes, where they have survived, often look moth-eaten and bedraggled, but originally they must have seemed very splendid, and there is evidence that the royal household maintained domestics called feather dressers whose main task was to keep the plumes in good order. 'The bedchambers ought all to have a fit place for the standing of their beds, remote from the blowings of doors and windows, and not far from the fire', remarks Pratt thoughtfully.

In the houses of the great the main bedchamber now often formed part of a suite of state rooms, all on the same floor (for it was customary to grant interviews or chat with friends either whilst actually in bed or else while dressing). Planning continued to be essentially balanced and regular. 'Beautiful it will be if all the great rooms be placed just in the middle, and afterwards that those on each hand of them have alike positions and also dimensions, as we find it to be in our own bodies, so that you shall see nothing on the one side which you shall not find to be answered by its like on the other', says Pratt, though as usual he advances a practical reason as well as an aesthetic one: 'for so will the roof lie much better upon the whole when each member bears its weight in so just a proportion.'

However, in all but the largest houses at this time there was a strong movement towards much smaller, more intimate apartments which gave a feeling of increased warmth and comfort. In fact the average country house was now being planned like a compact box, rather than as a long string of interconnected rooms. Pratt had designed Coleshill on what he called a 'double pile' plan, meaning that it was two rooms deep with a central corridor between them running the length of the house. This was almost revolutionary; up till then most smaller houses, and many larger ones, had been only one room deep, and the only way to get from one end of a house to the other was through the various rooms. The idea of corridors and passages, which to us seems so obvious, was in fact highly novel. Yet once generally accepted it made all the difference to the planning, interior convenience and comfort of a house. Once again, however, Pratt advances a social reason for his ideas: 'Let the whole [house] . . . be so furnished with back stairs and passages to them, that the ordinary servants may never publicly appear in passing to and fro for their occasion there'. Ham

26   *Chatsworth, Derbyshire, 1686–1707. State bedroom with ceiling and coving painted by Laguerre – note the* trompe l'oeil *figures complete with their painted shadows*

House is a positive warren of such concealed passages.

But we shall look in vain for bathrooms. On 21 February 1665 Samuel Pepys writes: 'My wife . . . busy in going with her woman to a hot-house to bath herself, after her long being within doors in the dirt, so that she now pretends to a resolution of being hereafter very clean. How long it will hold I can guess', he adds cynically, and in fact bathing is not mentioned again in the Diary. However, there were public hot baths in London and some other cities, for one of which establishments Mrs Pepys was evidently bound, and in fact a few large houses did have rooms specially set apart for bathing in portable tubs (there is one such room in the basement at Ham). As for sanitation, Pepys kept what he describes as a 'very fine close-stool' in his sitting room, and there was a cess-pit under his cellar floor. Since in this he was typical of his age, further comment is unnecessary.

In other matters, however, he was more forward-looking. 'In the morning . . . comes Sympson to set up my other new press for my books', he writes on 24 August 1666. These presses were free-standing bookcases, among the earliest of their kind, almost certainly the earliest to be documented, and still surviving at Pepys's old Cambridge college of Magdalene, together with some 3,000 of his books. They are oak cupboards with glazed doors, the upper part standing on a slightly projecting base whose front is also glazed. However, they cannot have been unique, for other very similar examples were made for Dyrham Court (Gloucestershire), and these too are still extant.

In the same passage Pepys goes on to tell how he and Sympson 'fell in to the furnishing of my new closet . . . and so all the afternoon, till it was quite dark hanging things, that is, my maps and picture[s] . . . and setting up my books, and as much as we could do, to my most extraordinary satisfaction; so that I think it will be as noble a closet as any hath, and light enough; though indeed, it would be better to have had a little more light.' Such a private sanctum is typical of the more intimate note that was creeping into the life-style of the seventeenth century in all except the most exalted households, where formality was still the order of the day. And though rooms in town houses such as Pepys's had always been smaller on average than those in country houses, owing to lack of space, yet even at Ham House the library, despite its title and book shelves, is no more than a closet.

In such surroundings it was now possible to relax, perhaps in one of the still rather rare upholstered chairs with high back, draught-deterring 'cheeks' (wings) and thick, loose squab cushions in the seat; such chairs are first recorded in the latter part of the seventeenth century. Among the ultimate in luxurious comfort must have been the '2 sleeping chayres, carv'd and guilt frames, covered with crimson and gould stuff with gould fringe' which are recorded in an inventory of 1679 at Ham, where they may still be seen. In fact they are ornate wing armchairs with moveable backs which can be adjusted by means of ratchets. The head-rest of the day-bed, in use until about 1700, could now also be adjusted, usually by means of small chains. At the Restoration the day-bed was made in the same style as the chairs of the period; the frame was often of walnut, the stretchers turned and carved, and cane panels were used for the seat and back. By the end of the century, however, it was ornate, upholstered, and soon to be supplanted by the couch proper.

Bodily comfort was also promoted by the introduction of the settee, somewhere about the 1680s. At first it had a tall, double-arched back, and in fact looked like two of the early wing armchairs joined together with the centre arms missing. Cane was again used in seats and backs, though more expensive examples were upholstered and covered, like the wing armchairs, with damask, velvet or embroidery.

The later post-Restoration period is notable for the considerable amount of case-furniture – bureaux, cabinets and the like – that began to be made, again as part of the movement towards a more conveniently personal kind of life-style. More people now had sufficient interest, time and money to begin collecting art objects such as coins, medals, miniatures and jewellery, and to house such treasures a variety of large cabinets were made, mostly with a number of small drawers hidden behind two hinged doors, the whole resting on a stand with barley sugar twist-turned legs. These were already widely produced during the reign of Charles II. Another newcomer was the writing cabinet with drawers, pigeon-holes and a fall front forming a desk surface; this cabinet too rested on a stand. A refinement of the 1690s was the escritoire, essentially a box with a sloping lid on a gate-legged stand which could support the lid when this was opened to form a writing surface.

Originally the walnut or other woods from which such pieces were made was used in the solid – an expensive business, especially in the case of walnut. The accession of William and Mary of Orange in 1689 meant that the influx of Continental craftsmen (especially Dutch), which from 1660 on had been something of a gentle trickle, now became a flood. It had already been greatly augmented after 1685 by the arrival of many Huguenot craftsmen, following Louis XIV's revocation of the Edict of Nantes in that year, an action which removed the official protection hitherto enjoyed by French Protestants. In the field of furniture these immigrants not only brought the term 'cabinet-maker' into our language (it first appears about 1695), but also new skills, designs and techniques, above all those of veneering and marquetry.

In the technique of veneering, thinly-cut sheets of wood are glued over the main body (called the carcase) of a piece of furniture, so as to conceal it completely; thus, for example, a veneer of walnut can be laid over a carcase of pine or deal, making the piece look as though it were made of solid walnut, though at a much smaller cost. Nowadays sheets of veneer are cut very thinly by machine, and have been since the nineteenth century, but originally they had to be cut by hand and were on average about one-eighth of an inch thick.

It is normal to arrange the different sheets of veneer so that an overall pattern

27 *Panelled room, about 1685, from a house in London. Though this is a town house, the room has about it a feeling of comfortable snugness equally applicable to country houses of the period. (V. and A. Museum)*

is obtained from the grain, and this is often of great beauty. Indeed it seems that the earliest version of the word was 'faneer', perhaps because of the fan-shaped pattern that could be made (Evelyn, in *Sylvia*, speaks of 'faneering, as they term it'). One of the most effective designs is called 'oyster veneer' because of its resemblance to oyster shells; each piece is obtained by cutting through the smaller branches of a tree – usually laburnum or olive – at an angle. Some veneers look best when the sheets are cut from the growths or burrs that grow on the roots and trunks of trees where these have suffered damage; this is especially true of walnut, whose grain is otherwise rather uninteresting.

Veneering was of course especially suitable for case-furniture of all types, as well as a means of saving money. For not only could the carcase of a piece be made much more cheaply, but it was not necessary to veneer the back at all, as most such pieces were intended to stand against a wall. This is why most of them are rough and unfinished on their fourth, hidden side. Despite superb craftsman-ship our prudent forefathers saw no reason to squander money needlessly. Unfortunately they did not then realise that by gluing the boards of the pinewood carcase together they had allowed it no room for natural expansion, with the result that many a fine veneer has cracked and split as the planks to which it is glued have moved apart.

Marquetry, though originating in France, also reached us via Holland at about the same time as veneering, of which it is in fact a decorative form. In marquetry, woods of different colours (some natural, some induced by staining) are cut out in a fretwork-like manner and assembled so as to produce a picture or pattern, somewhat as in the technique of inlay (see p. 19); however, in the case of marquetry the pieces of wood are glued to the surface of the carcase, not let into it as with inlay. The Dutch were especially fond of simulating fruit and flowers in marquetry, and at first the English followed their lead. But as time went on the work of the English craftsmen surpassed that of their contemporaries in Holland, while the actual pieces of wood they used are much smaller, and there are many more of them to each object portrayed. (The art of marquetry was, however, to reach the highest pitch of its development in eighteenth-century France.) Marquetry, as well as plain veneering, was much used on case-furniture of the later seventeenth and early eighteenth centuries, as well as on such areas as the tops of side-tables. In addition to floral marquetry, seaweed marquetry (so called because it is made up from small pieces whose shape resembles fronds of seaweed) was also popular. Marquetry in general fell into disfavour during the mid-eighteenth century and though to some extent re-introduced in or about the 1780s was not executed with quite such devoted care; much fine 'marquetry' of the late eighteenth century will in fact be seen, on close inspection, to have been drawn in with pen and ink.

Returning now for a moment to the theme of privacy, it is interesting to notice, towards the end of the seventeenth century, the increasing provision of small dressing tables with drawers and recesses to hold the surprisingly large quantities of cosmetics and toilet articles used at that time. In fact toilet sets containing brushes and other implements, boxes and jars of many shapes and sizes had been in vogue ever since 1660, the more luxurious of them covered in silver. Men also used cosmetics, though the dressing tables would seem to have been primarily for the use of ladies. The drawer fronts are sometimes delicately concaved, and the handles are the small drop-shaped ones typical of the period; secured hopefully through the drawerfronts on the simple split-pin principle, they have all too often come adrift and been lost, to be replaced by others of a later date.

A necessary corollary to fashionable toilet is a mirror, and with the dressing tables of the period we find the first swing mirrors on simple stands which also often incorporate small drawers. Mirror glass had been originally imported from Venice, despite sporadic attempts (some fairly successful) to produce it here. However, soon after 1660 the Duke of Buckingham was granted a patent to begin regular production in a glassworks at Vauxhall. To begin with the plates were very small, and by 1670 were still only about three feet long. For hanging, mirror glass was placed in square or oblong frames to which were sometimes added decorative semicircular crests; the frames could be carved, veneered, decorated with marquetry or covered with beaten silver according to one's taste and purse. The plates themselves were thin and were backed by raw silver which, if touched or jarred, has a tendency to come away leaving a blotched surface. By the end of the seventeenth century, when glass had become cheaper, the frames were taller and narrower; however it was still not possible to make the plates sufficiently large, so two were used, one large and another about half its size. The joining of the two plates is clearly visible about two-thirds of the way up the frame, while a single large plate in a frame of the period must mean that the glass is a modern replacement. This rule holds good until the later eighteenth century. Moreover, the earlier the glass, the less perceptible to the eye is the bevel on the edge of the plate.

From about 1670 mirror glass was used as an alternative to paintings in fireplace overmantels. These were now sometimes constructed with a variety of small shelves and projections for the display of blue-and-white Delftware and Chinese porcelain, the collecting of which had become fashionable; it was also housed in special alcoves set into the panelled walls, and even small rooms designated as 'china closets' were allocated to it (there is one at Knole). The larger bowls and vases were apparently massed on the tops of cabinets in a way that to us looks untidy but to our ancestors must have seemed perfectly logical.

Further point was given to this kind of arrangement when, as often happened, the cabinet itself was in the popular lacquered finish associated with the Far East. There is some evidence of interest in oriental lacquer work during early Stuart and even Tudor times, but its true popularity dates from 1660 onwards. With the Restoration came a sudden fascination for Eastern art, at first called 'Indian' without any kind of distinction; here was yet another manifestation of the luxurious and the exotic (already popular on the Continent and especially in France), which was seized upon by a society hungry for such things. The arrival of tea helped to stimulate this interest, and so did the importation by the East India Company of lacquered chests and other objects from China. These rapidly became so fashionable that demand outran supply, and quite soon chests and cabinets were being both made and lacquered here at home.

True lacquer is the resin of a tree which does not grow in our latitudes, and as it hardens on exposure to the air it could not be imported. A substitute therefore had to be invented, and took the form of a mixture of whitening and size applied in several separate coats and varnished, the varnish itself being coloured by the addition of substances such as lamp-black and then highly polished. A raised design could be obtained from a paste made from whitening, gum arabic and size which was built up to the required depth over the outlines of the design. These techniques were expounded in a famous early book on the subject, *A Treatise of Japanning and Varnishing* published in 1688 by John Stalker and

George Parker. The terms 'japan' and 'lac' were used, rather than lacquer. * It is usually fairly easy to distinguish quickly between genuine Oriental designs and those conceived and executed in Europe, for the latter are comparatively crude and the various motifs are all mixed up in a way which no true Chinese artist would ever approve. A clue to the general insensitivity of our forefathers towards Oriental art, despite their enthusiasm for it, is supplied by the way in which they cut up panels of lacquer designs (especially those which formed the wings of imported screens) to form veneer surfaces for mirror frames, cabinets and so on; the pieces so cut were usually reassembled haphazardly, not making a coherent overall design.

The large lacquered chests and cabinets were normally placed on very highly-carved and gilded or (more usually) silvered stands of wood made especially to fit them, and sometimes also had equally ostentatious ornamental crests of carved wood placed on top, to add to the general air of opulence. But the process of lacquering was also applied to more everyday objects such as chairs, bureaux and day-beds. It was easy to do, and all too soon became the province of the amateur; by the 1690s it was being taught to girls as a fashionable time-waster. Despite some fluctuation in popularity it persisted as a means of decoration until the nineteenth century. However, it is the great lacquered chests and cabinets on their splendid stands that epitomise perhaps better than anything else the new richness and luxury that first entered English homes at the time of the Restoration.

As the seventeenth century merged into the eighteenth, little general change was to be observed in the styles of house building. The term 'Queen Anne' is today still used indiscriminately but understandably for houses which on investigation are shown to date from the seventeenth century, though Anne actually reigned from 1702 until 1714.

However, the period of transition is distinguished and enlivened by the unique contribution made to English domestic architecture by Sir John Vanbrugh (1664–1726). This colourful character had been soldier, gentleman of fortune and successful playwright before turning his hand quite suddenly, and apparently without any practical experience, to architecture – a good illustration of the somewhat casual attitude towards that branch of the arts which often prevailed in those days, though there is nothing casual about Vanbrugh's work. We know that he assisted the ageing Wren in the building of Greenwich Hospital and Kensington Palace, but not exactly to what extent. He himself built only a small number of houses, but several of these were of huge proportions (though not all were completed) and the largest of them all is Blenheim.

Begun in 1705, Blenheim Palace was originally conceived less as a home for the Duke and Duchess of Marlborough than as a sort of national shrine, and

* 'A Jappanian work is anything Jappaned, or Varnished, China-polished or the like' (*The Closet of Beauty*, a little book about cosmetics, etc., 1694).

28 *Lacquered cabinet on a stand of carved and silvered wood, with detachable crest to match. Late seventeenth century. (V. and A. Museum)*

indeed Vanbrugh himself declared that he 'look'd upon it much more as an intended monument to the Queen's glory than as a private habitation for the Duke' – which was fine for the Queen but not so satisfactory for the Duke. Certainly its monumental scale is matched only by its monumental discomforts, and it has been aptly called 'a stone monument with rooms contrived within for the convenience of its custodians'.* The story of Vanbrugh's work at Blenheim is a long one of constant quarrels with Sarah, the redoubtable Duchess of Marlborough; though the funds, originally supplied from the royal purse, dwindled and eventually dried up as the Marlboroughs fell out of royal favour and into political obscurity, Vanbrugh was unwilling to sacrifice any part of his grand design for mere financial reasons, and eventually he was dismissed from the site and banned from entering the grounds.

Vanbrugh's houses contain elements of medieval Gothic architecture as well as Renaissance classicism and the Pratt/May style, and he owes an obvious debt to Wren. However, it is not so much the various architectural features themselves as the ways in which Vanbrugh uses them that is so distinctive, for he mixes all the features together in a manner which other, more conventional architects must have considered almost revolutionary. The chief impression produced by a Vanbrugh building on the average visitor is one of enormous pressure and mass – 'mighty forces opposing overwhelming weights', as Sir Nikolaus Pevsner puts it.† Vanbrugh also introduced some entirely new ideas; for instance, Castle Howard in Yorkshire (begun 1699) is the first domestic dwelling in this country to have a dome, as distinct from a church or other public building.

Vanbrugh's style, sometimes known as English Baroque, is so individual that those architects of importance who followed his lead can be counted on the fingers of one hand. They included Thomas Archer (1668–1743), who built the arresting church of St John in Smith Square, London, and Nicholas Hawksmoor (1661–1736), a genius in his own right but whose fate too often has been to be overshadowed by both Wren and Vanbrugh, whose Clerk of Works he was. It was Hawksmoor who completed the work at Blenheim after Vanbrugh's dismissal. Easton Neston (Northamptonshire) is the only country house which can be fully credited to Hawksmoor, who was at his best and most inspired as a builder of London churches, notably St Mary Woolnoth near the Bank of England, and the magnificent Christ Church, Spitalfields, derelict ever since the Second World War and, as such, a standing reproach to the authorities of both Church and State.‡

* S. Sitwell, *British architects and craftsmen*, p. 92. 1945.
† *An outline of European architecture*, p. 571. 1960. In speaking of Vanbrugh one should never ignore his earlier links with the theatre, for Blenheim is nothing if not entirely theatrical in its conception.
‡ It is only fair to state that a partial restoration has now been carried out, which enables concerts and other events (though not regular services) to take place in Christ Church.

CHAPTER THREE

Palladian Formality

D URING the early years of the eighteenth century a remarkable change came over country house building and decoration. The year 1715 is of especial importance, for during it a previously obscure Scottish architect named Colen Campbell (who seems to have trained originally as a lawyer) published, in a folio volume, a collection of engravings showing British seventeenth- and early eighteenth-century houses and other buildings. He also provided a preface about architecture in which he not only pays rather perfunctory lip-service to living architects such as Vanbrugh and Wren but, more significantly, loudly sings the praises of 'the great Palladio, who has exceeded all that were gone before him and surpassed his contemporaries, whose ingenious labours will eclipse many and rival most of the Ancients'.

It is unclear exactly why or how Campbell (d. 1729) first became interested in the ideas and works of Palladio. But this interest inevitably extended to Inigo Jones, and led to Campbell's calling his publication *Vitruvius Britannicus*, 'The British Vitruvius', in homage to Jones whom Campbell and his friends recognised as the first British apostle of both the Roman Vitruvius and of Palladio. The work eventually ran to three volumes before Campbell died in 1729.

Campbell, however, was not merely a theorist but a practising architect as well (some of his own designs are included in *Vitruvius Britannicus*), and he proceeded to build houses of an Italianate classicism distilled from a mixture of Palladio and Jones. His first important house, Wanstead in Essex (begun 1715), was demolished in 1824, but contemporary engravings show that it was very large and that the façade was dominated by the first of those great temple-like porches or porticos without which almost no country house in the new style was to be thought complete. (However, there is an even earlier attempt at such a portico, though on a smaller scale, at The Vyne, Hampshire; this is probably by John Webb, Jones's kinsman, and dates from about 1654.) These porticos, projecting from the centre of the main façade, usually consist of a huge pediment supported at the front on a row of columns, with a single or double flight of steps leading up to the entrance at first floor level.

In its own day Wanstead was tremendously influential, but of all Campbell's houses it is the strangely-named Mereworth Castle (near Tonbridge, Kent) that catches the public imagination. Moreover Mereworth still stands, although unfortunately it is not at present open to visitors. Anything less like a castle it would be hard to imagine, but in fact the name was that of an earlier moated and fortified manor house which originally stood on the spot. Campbell's Mereworth is a completely symmetrical square house with a central dome and a pillared portico on each of the four sides. Nothing like it had been seen in England before, although several imitations followed. But it had an excellent Italian model, a villa standing just outside Vicenza and built in the 1550s by none other than Palladio himself. This house, known variously as the Villa Rotonda or the Villa Capra, is also perfectly regular in plan and has a domed central area, though the dome is less pronounced than Campbell's. It too has four porticos, each with its flight of steps; at Mereworth only two of the porticos, at opposite sides of the house, have steps, but this was due to the presence of the original moat which was not filled in until the nineteenth century.

Mereworth is thus our first surviving country house to show so obviously and so strongly the direct influence of Andrea Palladio on architectural thought in England. Campbell built a number of other important houses, such as Stourhead in Wiltshire (1721), the first example of the smaller country house in the new style, and Houghton Hall in Norfolk (1722), built for Sir Robert Walpole, which with its four domed corner blocks owes something to Jones's Wilton. In fact, although Mereworth will always remain Campbell's most

29   *Mereworth Castle, Kent. By Colen Campbell, 1723. The pavilion on the right is one of two that were built later to accommodate a larger staff*

striking memorial, in the long term it is Houghton and Wanstead which may be said to have had the most influence. Meanwhile a useful corrective to the mistaken belief that Campbell and his contemporaries were unable to design anything on an intimate scale is Ebberston Hall (Yorkshire), built by Campbell in 1718. This is a tiny, scaled-down version of the large mansions – Houghton or Mereworth viewed through the wrong end of a telescope, as it were – in which the proportions of the rooms and details of the decoration are reduced accordingly. The result is enchanting.

Led by Campbell, and reinforced by the publication in 1715 not only of *Vitruvius Britannicus* but also of an important English edition of Palladio's *Four Books of Architecture*, the new architectural movement gathered momentum and gained the title Palladianism by which it has ever since been known, while those who followed it are called the Palladians. The movement embraced many famous names, but apart from that of Campbell himself two others are outstanding. They are those of Lord Burlington and William Kent.

No discussion of eighteenth-century art can be complete without some reference to the importance of the Grand Tour. This was the social tradition, already long established, by which the sons of noblemen and gentlemen were sent to Europe, and especially to Italy, to study the customs and art of the various countries they visited in the company of their tutors and servants. The

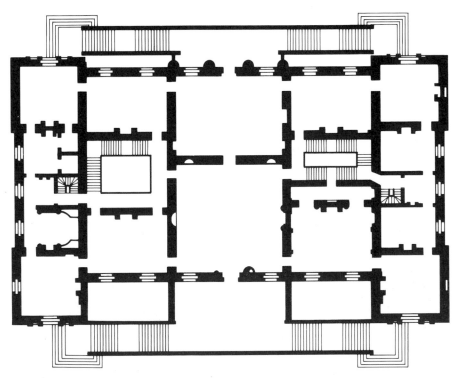

30 *Plan of Houghton Hall, Norfolk. By Colen Campbell, 1722–31. Almost total symmetry deriving ultimately from Palladio but via Inigo Jones*

prevalence of this tradition greatly helped to spread the Palladian architectural doctrine at home. Richard Boyle, third Earl of Burlington, was born in 1694 and succeeded to his title at the early age of ten; he made the Grand Tour twice, in 1714 and again in 1719. After the first he employed Campbell to remodel his London home, Burlington House in Piccadilly, now much altered and the home of the Royal Academy of Arts. The second tour, already greatly influenced by Campbell's ideas, he made with the express intention of buying up as many of Palladio's original designs as he could find, and of seeing as many of Palladio's buildings as possible. He was also careful to study original Roman remains at first hand.

The outstanding result of this second tour was the famous Chiswick Villa which Burlington designed himself and built during 1725–26. It was not primarily intended to be lived in, since at the time there stood nearby the family's old Jacobean mansion (demolished in 1788), but as a combined paintings and sculpture gallery, for during his travels Lord Burlington had amassed numerous works of art as well as a large collection of drawings by Inigo Jones and others, to say nothing of those by Palladio, and he needed extra space in which to house them. Some critics, however, could see little or no use for the Villa at all; Lord Hervey acidly summed it up as being 'Too small to live in, and too large to hang to one's watch.'

The Villa was obviously strongly influenced both by Palladio's Villa Rotonda and by Campbell's Mereworth, for it too has a symmetrically square outline plan and a domed central area. But there are important differences – a single portico, the dome on an octagonal base instead of a round one, and so on –

31 *Stourhead, Wiltshire. By Colen Campbell, 1722, but not completed to his design until the nineteenth century*

32   *Chiswick House, London. By Lord Burlington, 1725. The impressive double staircase is more elaborate than strictly Palladian*

which show that Burlington was an architect in his own right and not just an imitator of other people's ideas. Above all, he became the acknowledged leader of the Palladian movement, the principal theorist, the man to whom all the other landed gentry turned for advice when they decided to build or rebuild in the Palladian style. For the times were peculiarly ripe for an outburst of such building. The whole political atmosphere had changed in 1714 with the accession of George I and the replacement of the Tories by the Whigs. The ruling and landed classes wished to turn their backs on anything that smacked of the Stuart era, including the architectural styles of men such as Wren and Vanbrugh, and were now ready and willing to accept that classical manner of building which in the time of Inigo Jones they had for the most part decisively rejected. At Chiswick the change is symbolised, as it were, by the presence beside the portico of Rysbrack's statues of Jones and Palladio, confronting the visitor like the tutelary deities that guard the entrance to a Japanese temple.

Returning from his second Italian tour, Lord Burlington brought with him an English painter who for some years had been working in Rome. This was William Kent (?1685–1748), a Yorkshireman of humble origin and at first a coach-painter, who had been sent to Rome by a consortium of wealthy patrons for whom, in return for financial support while he studied painting, he bought up works of art and despatched them to his patrons' homes in England. He also acted as guide and advisor to the many English visitors in Rome, and it was no doubt in this capacity that he and Burlington originally met. Kent was something of a genius, combining in himself (as later transpired) the talents of painter, architect, furniture designer, interior decorator and landscape gardener. Moreover he was soon brought fully into sympathy with the aims and ideals of the Palladian movement, and became Burlington's right-hand man. After the return from Italy he became a permanent member of the Burlington household (which for a short time also included George Frederick Handel) and never left it until his death in 1748. Few human relationships can have been more bizarre than the evidently deep and lasting friendship between the jovial, extrovert and lowly-born Kent, noted for his unfailing good humour, and the somewhat cold, introspective and blue-blooded Burlington. It survived Burlington's marriage, and contained nothing of homosexuality. Nevertheless it is clear that theirs was a true partnership, not a subservient master-to-man relationship, and it led to the building of a typically great mansion, Holkham Hall in Norfolk. Holkham is sometimes attributed to Kent alone, but he is unlikely to have completed the designs without reference to the owner Thomas Coke, Earl of Leicester (himself a deeply committed Palladian, whom Kent had first met years earlier in Rome) and above all to Burlington, who as Kent's patron had procured for his protégé several lucrative official posts under the Crown.

From Wanstead to Holkham and beyond, most of the great Palladian houses present us with the same basic characteristics. The main mass of the central block is flanked at each side by a wing, often attached to the central block by a connecting arm. Beyond the house proper may be additional stable and kitchen blocks, either entirely separate or else also linked to it by covered or semi-covered ways (the device of a roofed passage, with an open colonnade taking the place of one of the side walls, was popular). The entire composition is balanced and regular. At ground level the storey is normally 'rusticated', that is, the joints between the blocks of stone are heavily emphasised with extra-deep grooves so as to give a feeling of strength and solidity. Londoners can see a good example of a modified Palladian house by looking at the Horse Guards building in Whitehall, for this is said to be based on one of Kent's rejected designs for Holkham, though it was completed after his death.

In general the exteriors of Palladian houses seem perhaps rather severe, sometimes even stark. The strongly rhythmical façades with their evenly-spaced windows can appear strangely featureless, except for the great porticos with their heavy pediments and huge columns rising up through a height of two storeys. Inside, however, the tale is different. As though to compensate for the exteriors, the interiors are rich in colour and decoration, as indeed were those of Palladio and of Jones. Few are richer or more colourful than Chiswick, where the interior decoration was Kent's first important work of this kind for Lord Burlington and bears strong evidence of the Italian influence that he must have absorbed whilst in that country.

In one field of decorative art, however, Kent was the last important exponent and not, as in others, a pioneer. This was mural painting. When originally

33 *Holkham Hall, Norfolk. By William Kent, 1734, aided by Lords Burlington and Leicester. The portico is here placed on the garden front and is ornamental rather than practical*

taken under Burlington's wing Kent's profession had been that of a painter, and it was as a painter that he was first launched by his new patron. By means of backstairs politics, distasteful to us but entirely acceptable in the eighteenth century, Burlington obtained for Kent a commission to paint the ceilings of several of the state rooms in Kensington Palace, as well as the walls and ceilings of the main staircase there; this was in spite of the fact that by rights the task should have been assigned to the official court painter, Sir James Thornhill – but Thornhill was by then considered to be out of date and old-fashioned. Kent's work can still be seen at Kensington, the staircase in particular being quite an impressive restatement of an old formula (much used by Verrio, Laguerre and Thornhill), in which a crowd of painted spectators looks down from an architectural setting on to the living visitor. It is the more notable in that the figures are contemporary people in national costumes, not the usual classical gods; here Kent departs from tradition, though reverting to it again with an interesting self-portrait on the ceiling.

But there can be no dodging the fact that, while painting was one of Kent's many accomplishments, it was nevertheless the one in which he was least successful. Furthermore, the all-embracing 'all-over' style of mural decoration was no longer fashionable; it characterised a period which most people were trying to forget. And so it is not surprising that Kent's paintings at Kensington are virtually the last of their kind in England. What is more, except for the staircase, they are once again confined within the frames formed by the plaster compartments of the ceilings. This is also the case at Chiswick where there are other ceiling paintings, the most important being those by the Venetian artist Sebastiano Ricci, although Kent provided panels of painted decoration. He carried out another impressive scheme of decoration on the staircase at Houghton; this consists of simulated architecture and statuary mainly in grisaille (monochrome imitation of stone). However, according to Horace Walpole, this was because Sir Robert Walpole (Horace's father) had a low opinion of Kent's powers as a colourist. (Of Kent's portraits, Horace unkindly says that they 'bore little resemblance to the persons that sat for them; and the colouring was worse, more raw and undetermined than that of the most errant journeymen to the profession'.)*

The work of Kent apart, paintings ceased to be a regular feature of Palladian ceilings. The heavy plaster-clad beams remained, as in the preceding century, but the decorative mouldings were purged of all associations with naturalism and were normally entirely abstract. Since it is from these mouldings (very frequently gilded or otherwise picked out in colours) that Palladian interiors acquire much of that general sense of richness which they impart to the visitor, we ought here to consider them more closely.

---

*Walpole's various comments on Kent are to be found in his *Anecdotes of painting in England*, first published in 1780.

The mouldings in question are horizontal or vertical continuous bands of repeated motifs, the stock-in-trade of classical decoration, used originally on Greek and Roman public buildings but used by Renaissance architects, by Inigo Jones and by the Palladians on private houses as well, both inside and out. In a Palladian house mouldings in profusion, superimposed one above the other, not only decorate ceiling beams but form the friezes and cornices of rooms and the ornamentation of doors, windows, fireplaces, large pieces of furniture and so on. They may be executed in stone, wood or plaster (occasionally even simulated in paint) and are distinguished by names, of which the following are amongst those most frequently encountered:

ACANTHUS LEAF: Based on the toothed and jagged leaf of the acanthus plant; a very ancient and popular motif.

BAYLEAF GARLAND: A horizontal band of formal bayleaves with a criss-cross binding at regular intervals.

BEAD-AND-REEL: A sequence of alternating round and oblong shapes.

DENTIL: Three-dimensional teeth-like (hence the derivation) blocks, clearly separated from one another.

EGG-AND-DART, EGG-AND-TONGUE: Ovoid shapes alternating with vertical arrow- or spear-heads.

GREEK KEY OR MEANDER: An angular, maze-like pattern of which there are a number of variants.

VITRUVIAN WAVE OR SCROLL: A flowing pattern of curvilinear line.

Acanthus leaf

Bay leaf garland

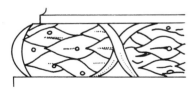

Bead and reel

Dentil

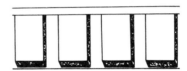

Egg and dart

Greek key or meander
(there are different
forms of this)

34 *Some of the more usual classical mouldings*

The Palladians' chief original source for the design of interior doorways was
Inigo Jones, Kent and Burlington having set the pattern at Chiswick where
they had ready to hand Burlington's own collection of Jones's drawings. Door-
frames are heavily carved with the various mouldings and the overdoor is
frequently in the form of an architectural pediment, often a 'broken' pediment
in which the central portion and apex of the triangle is cut out so as to leave a
shaped space in which a bust or other ornament was sometimes placed. Fireplaces too were often adapted from Jones, being bulky and architecturally
conceived, with the overmantel still forming an integral part of the whole,
surmounted by a pediment and framing a mirror or a painting. Marble panels
in high relief by contemporary sculptors such as Rysbrack were also sometimes
incorporated, marble being a common material for fireplaces in general.
Horace Walpole again criticises Kent in this connection, complaining that,
'His chimney-pieces, though lighter than those of Inigo, whom he imitated, are
frequently heavy; and his constant introduction of pediments and the members
of architecture over doors, and within rooms, was disproportioned and cum-
brous.'

Important though the various mouldings are to classical schemes of architecture and decoration, even more fundamental are the classical columns with
their different decorative capitals, or tops, each having its own name. The main
ones are:

DORIC: A column with totally plain capital.

IONIC: A capital with four slightly concave sides and at each corner a
downward-scrolled decoration (called a volute) reminiscent of a ram's
horn.

CORINTHIAN: A capital consisting of a naturalistic design of vertical acanthus
leaves.

These columns with their capitals were used by the ancients as basic ingredients of their architecture, and are known as the 'Orders of architecture'.
To the Renaissance architects who learned about them from Vitruvius they
came as a revelation. Strict rules regarding their proportions and usage, also
found to some extent in Vitruvius, were re-interpreted by Palladio, and an
additional Order called the Composite was revived, in which the capital was
formed from Ionic volutes superimposed above Corinthian acanthus leaves.
(The ancient Greeks had slightly different versions of the Orders; these were
not known to the Renaissance, and did not appear in this country until the
eighteenth century.)

Only rarely are the Orders of structural importance in a Palladian house,
except in the portico where they support the pediment. Pilasters are entirely
ornamental, though of equal decorative importance. These are square-section
columns attached to a wall and partly projecting from it; they share the same
sequence of capitals as do the columns proper.

All this may seem rather learned and unnecessary, but to Inigo Jones and later to the Palladians it was the very stuff of their architecture. One cannot examine a Palladian house for long, either inside or out, without becoming aware of the importance of the classical columns in the general scheme of building, and so it is as well to understand why this is so, even though one may not always remember the different names of the Orders.

The most important rooms of Italian Renaissance palaces and villas are not normally at ground level but on the first floor, which is known as the 'piano nobile' (literally, 'stately storey'). This arrangement was not unknown in England even in the sixteenth century (for example, at Osterley House, completed in its original state by 1576), and was of course followed by Jones, as any visitor to Wilton, the Queen's House or the Banqueting House will soon notice. But the Palladians were the first to carry it out on a large scale, and in following the idea they had a practical as well as a decorative reason for introducing the imposing porticos with their flights of steps leading up to the first floor, for it was on that floor that the main entrance hall was now usually situated. For the hall at Houghton Campbell adopted Inigo Jones's 40-foot cube, a feature also repeated in other Palladian houses such as Clandon Park in Surrey (the work of Giacomo Leoni, an immigrant Venetian who helped to prepare the 1715 English edition of Palladio's book). Among Palladian entrance halls highly original examples such as that at Holkham are unusual. Kent and Burlington based the plan of the Holkham hall on that of a Roman basilica (judgement

35   *Chiswick House. The Gallery, showing fine Venetian window (r.), richly coffered half-dome over an apse, and a profusion of classical mouldings*

hall), with pillared aisles and a semicircular or apsidal end. But at Holkham the grand entrance stairs are *inside* the hall, rising up within the apse to first-floor level, while the unpretentious front door is at ground level and the inevitable portico becomes a purely ornamental feature on the garden side of the house. (Walpole says that Kent originally intended to place a gigantic statue of Jupiter at the head of the stairs, which would of course have completed the temple-like appearance of the hall.)

At Holkham the ceiling of the hall is partly 'coffered' – that is, decorated with geometrically-shaped recessed panels arranged in regular patterns; the shapes decrease in size towards the top of the ceiling or dome, giving an optical illusion of perspective. This coffering was also an ancient form of Roman decoration, and early Palladian usage of it occurs at Chiswick where Burlington introduced it in conjunction with another Roman feature, a half-dome sur-mounting an apse at cornice level. He must himself have seen, whilst in Rome, ruined classical temples and other buildings in which such coffered half-domes were still to be found. No doubt the Chiswick coffering was introduced in consultation with Kent, who had already decorated the dome of one of the state rooms at Kensington Palace with coffering simulated in paint. However, it is normally executed in plaster, as at Chiswick, and is usually partly or wholly gilded. Sometimes entire ceilings were coffered, as in the Saloon at Holkham, where again Kent was responsible for the decorations.

Returning again to the average Palladian entrance hall (if so fine an apartment can be called average), we shall find it flagged with stone or marble. We shall probably *not* find the main staircase there, but instead tucked away behind or to one side, in an inner hall. In their anxiety to adhere to the system of 'harmonic proportions' and to make interior planning as regular and balanced as possible, the Palladians tended to place functional items such as staircases, which might disrupt the general symmetry, into corners where they were likely to do least damage to the grand design. Perhaps the most extreme instance of this is at Chiswick, where interior communication between the ground and first floors was by means of four narrow spiral staircases neatly concealed in the supporting walls of the central dome.

The staircase, when found, will often be of stone or marble and in many instances will have an iron balustrade. It is more austere than the average staircase of the later seventeenth century, which in general is of wood and has a broad heavily-moulded handrail over turned balusters which stand on the outer string (the board that runs on its edge parallel to the treads). In eighteenth-century houses the balusters stand on the treads themselves. (There is a certain type of seventeenth-century staircase which has heavily-carved and pierced infilling of foliage, military accoutrements, etc. instead of balusters, and in which the newel posts are topped by carved wooden baskets of fruit and flowers; examples are at Ham House, Sudbury Hall, and Thrumpton Hall, Nottingham-shire.)

Behind and around the hall the principal rooms are arranged in stately sequence and lit by tall windows, among which the Venetian or Palladian window (see p. 36) takes pride of place, forming important punctuation points in the façades and being also a useful trademark of the style.

In planning their houses the Palladian architects did not usually pay much attention to comfort and convenience. The kitchens, for example, were often placed at what we today would consider a ridiculous distance from the dining rooms, sometimes in wings or pavilions detached from the main block of the house and reached only by covered ways, subterranean passages, or even across open courtyards. There is no doubt that much of the hot food intended for our ancestors was tepid before it reached the table; yet equally there is no doubt that such small inconveniences were philosophically endured in the cause of art. Nobody would have dreamed of grumbling. The main thing was that the principal storey should present the visitor with a gracious and ordered sequence of perfectly-proportioned rooms which together should add up to a textbook of Palladian planning and decoration. In such a scheme of things mere bodily needs came a poor second, and so did complete privacy; it was still accepted that the main bedrooms should be on the same floor as the reception rooms and be interconnected with them. The Palladian attitude is in this sense a regression from that of the later seventeenth century, which as we have seen was in some respects moving towards a more intimate view of domestic life.

As the modern visitor sets out from the entrance hall to walk through the various state rooms of a Palladian house, he will sooner or later notice the great side-tables standing against the walls. These were now found in most rooms of importance and their function had become almost entirely ornamental. Almost all have massive marble slab tops – a custom of Italian origin, though the marble is sometimes an imitation known as scagliola. Some have front legs only and are screwed to the wall at the back; the correct name for these is console table (console being the architectural term for a bracket). The word, however, soon came to denote all large side-tables of this type including those with four legs. Another name for them is pier table; in architecture a pier is the wall-space between two apertures, and the table is frequently placed against the wall between windows.

With these tables will frequently be found large mirrors, designed *en suite* (i.e., as a matching set), though with the glass still having to be made up from two separate plates, clearly visible to the eye. The decoration is florid, the table itself often very bulky, and the group of table-cum-mirror typifies the age just as surely as do the great lacquer cabinets of the later seventeenth century. For it is in such pieces that Palladian influence in general and that of William Kent in particular is most clearly shown.

As a furniture designer Kent was influenced less by pure Palladian ideals, to which he pays little more than lip-service in the form of classical mouldings, than by seventeenth-century Italian and especially Venetian furniture that he had seen and known while living in Italy. Again we see that the sober exteriors of Palladian houses conceal interiors and furnishings of great colour and richness. Into his pieces (designed for houses such as Houghton and Chiswick) Kent, with that enormous exuberance and panache that characterised everything he did, poured all the various decorative devices associated with Palladianism plus a number of others, notably the curious scroll-like legs that he uses on tables and settees, often ornamenting them with a shallow surface patterning like fish scales. Between the legs of his chairs, tables and settees hang great hammock-like loops and swags made up of fruit, flowers, husks and foliage, carved in wood or modelled in plaster and then gilded and/or painted white. Eagles with outstretched wings form the supports of console tables instead of legs, masks of satyrs and goddesses top mirror frames or act as chair-arm terminals, and Kent's favourite decorative device seems to have been the scallop shell, which he sometimes enlarged to huge proportions, as on the great dining table now at Chatsworth or the state bed at Houghton.

Kent's influence was enormous. 'His oracle was so much consulted by all who affected taste, that nothing was thought compleat without his assistance. He was not only consulted for furniture, as frames of pictures, glasses, tables, chairs &c. but for plate, for a barge, for a cradle. And so impetuous was fashion, that two great ladies prevailed on him to make designs for their birthday gowns. The one he dressed in a petticoat decorated with columns of the . . . Orders; the other like a bronze, in a copper-coloured satin with ornaments of gold' (Walpole; the barge, incidentally, was the royal one now in the National Maritime Museum at Greenwich). We should not therefore be surprised at the very considerable extent to which Kent's personal influence is reflected in the furniture of the period.

At the same time it is important to recognise that furniture actually designed by William Kent and his immediate associates was mostly intended to go into specific Palladian houses, and really only looks its best in those settings for which it was designed. (Indeed Kent is the first English architect of distinction to have provided furniture and fittings for his own houses.) Though magnificent, it is 'often unmeasurably ponderous', to borrow a phrase of Horace Walpole's, and was in any case far too expensive and eccentric for the average householder. It would be wrong to assume that the Kentian school of thought had no influence on the ordinary furniture of the time (and by ordinary I mean here pieces which, though fashionable, did not go to extremes). Generally speaking, though, that influence comes out most strongly in pieces which were more ornamental than functional, such as the side-tables, mirror frames and candlestands. These last were simply portable platforms which stood about the various rooms and on which were placed single or branched candlesticks, or perfume burners. Such burners were very acceptable on crowded social occasions at a time when, to put it as kindly as possible, standards of bodily cleanli-

36 *Houghton Hall. The Saloon, with ceiling paintings, chairs and stools all by Kent*

ness were not as high as they are today. Lord Hervey, in a letter to Walpole written in 1776, is not at all kind: 'At court last night there was dice, dancing, crowding, sweating and stinking in abundance as usual.'

The candlestands are often of pinewood, carved and gilded, and often also incorporate the Kent fish-scale scrolled support and a human head with or without torso, in imitation of ancient classical precedents; the head supports the platform, which is not infrequently in the shape of a classical capital.

Quite apart from the particular and individual influence of Kent, the furniture styles of the 1720s and '30s could not fail to be affected by the Palladian movement in general, then in full swing; indeed, during the first part of the eighteenth century the chief moulders of taste in furniture and decoration were in fact the architects. Thus much furniture of the period, especially large pieces such as bureaux, bookcases and so on, shows an architectural influence both in design and ornamentation. This had been apparent even before the Palladian era, in the typical walnut-veneered bureau-cum-cabinet, its top surmounted by a plain or broken pediment or by an arched section in the style of a Dutch gable. Cabinets such as these were made in three parts – a lower stage with drawers, a central bureau stage with fall front, small drawers and pigeon holes, and an upper cupboard stage with double doors, solid or faced with mirrors. Immediately below these doors one sometimes finds two little pull-out shelves. On these would be set candles which shed light onto the desk below; where there were mirror doors the amount of light would be increased by reflection. The original solid wooden ball or bun feet were replaced in popularity quite soon by shaped bracket supports.

The plain surfaces of such pieces were now enriched by pilasters and half-columns (i.e., columns split vertically and attached to a surface), by mouldings and friezes of dentil, Greek key, Vitruvian scroll, egg-and-dart and many other classical devices associated with the architecture of the time. It can be argued that wood ought not to be treated for decorative purposes as though it were stone, and inevitably there is a severe, angular look about much case-furniture of this period. On the other hand fashion was busily adopting a new wood which both in texture and appearance was much better suited to strong carving and hard outlines than walnut, though the latter continued to be used until mid-century. This new wood was mahogany.

The introduction of mahogany for furniture-making was originally due to a scarcity of imported Continental walnut, supplies of good English walnut having long ago become very limited. Prior to 1721 it was a little-known wood in this country, but in that year the lifting of duty on timber imported from British North America and the West Indies made it possible for the first Jamaican mahogany to be used; however, before long the main sources of supply were the former Spanish South American colonies of Cuba, San Domingo and Puerto Rico, the timber imported from these countries being known as Spanish mahogany. Its rich dark-red colour was new and compelling, so much so that some country craftsmen are said to have tried to get a similar effect by staining oak with bullocks' blood; moreover it was found that, unlike walnut, mahogany did not crack or warp, carved well, was stronger and more lasting, and was much more resistant to wood worm. (The predations of this dread insect, larva of the furniture beetle, are without doubt responsible for the destruction of much walnut furniture which might otherwise have survived to our own day. Oak is said to be fully resistant to the creature except in the sap streaks.) A further advantage enjoyed by mahogany was that the size of the trees made it possible for planks to be cut much larger than those of walnut. With all these points in its favour one is not surprised to find that by the late 1730s mahogany had established a long lead as the dominant wood for the making of fashionable furniture. Its first extensive use in any house for panelling seems to have been at Canons, Middlesex, the palatial mansion (later demolished) built between 1713 and 1720 for the Duke of Chandos.

At first mahogany furniture was made in the solid, but just as in the case of walnut this proved to be an expensive process and veneering was substituted. Legs of tables, chairs, settees and similar items of course continued to be made in the solid. Spanish mahogany is a heavy wood, and the weight of a suspect piece of early eighteenth century furniture such as a chair can be one factor in a snap decision as to whether in fact it is as early as it looks, or whether it is made of the lighter Honduras mahogany which was introduced later in the century.

It would be wrong to give the impression that all early mahogany furniture is designed in straight lines; in fact, in the case of chairs and settees the opposite is true. Changes in design, from the tall, upright, straight-backed chair of the later seventeenth century to something with a more flowing outline, had already been foreshadowed to some extent in the 1690s, notably in some of Daniel Marot's work. In a typical chair of about 1720–25 we shall find a new overall curving shape with a much lower back made up from two inward-curving outer supports and a flat central member or splat, shaped vaguely like a vase. The front of the seat is convex, the sides slightly concave. There are no stretchers. Later on, by the 1740s, the tendency was for the outline of seat and back to become square again, but the sense of flow and movement was not lost, for both styles of chair retained a distinguishing feature whose importance to furniture of the years 1720–40 can hardly be exaggerated. This was the cabriole leg with claw-and-ball foot.

The Oxford dictionary defines cabriole as 'a leap like that of a goat', and certainly the shape of this leg has about it the definite look of a quadruped's hind-quarters in the way that it swells outward at the knee, curves in again, and then begins a second outward curve just before it ends in the foot. Sometimes in early examples the goat analogy is pointed even more strongly by hoof-like feet. More usually, however, and more typically, the feet are claw-and-ball. It is thought that both the cabriole leg and the claw-and-ball foot may derive from imported Chinese furniture, and that the foot may have originated in the ancient Oriental motif of a dragon's claw holding a pearl (of wisdom). Whatever the truth of this, it is certain that earlier versions of this foot on English furniture are genuinely like the talons of a dragon or large bird of prey, though with the passage of time a hairy, lion-like paw was also introduced. The quality of a piece can sometimes be partly assessed by the degree of conviction with which the carver has shown the talons or claws to be grasping the ball.

Another characteristic of the cabriole leg at this period is that it tends to be fairly heavily carved on the knee, where the centrepiece of such carving is frequently a lion's mask. Other motifs that regularly appear there are the human or satyr mask and the cabuchon or 'uncut gem' device (a round, oval, or pear-shaped but otherwise plain protuberance). All these devices are normally framed in a setting of carved acanthus leaves, and all were of course carved from the solid wood of the leg; any shallowness about the carving or suggestion that it is cut into the leg instead of standing 'proud' must instantly raise suspicions that the faker has been at work.

Lion and human masks and eagles' heads were additionally popular at this time as the terminals of arms on settees and armchairs, which also shared the cabriole leg and claw-and-ball foot. (There devices were of course used by Kent and his followers, who absorbed them into their vocabulary of ornament.) The upholstered wing armchair was now firmly established in popularity, running on small castor wheels made from leather and having a loose squab cushion in the seat.

Cabriole leg and claw-and-ball foot were likewise applied to the various tables

37   *Design for a table for Houghton by Kent, dated 1731. The clerical caricatures are a typical Kentian* jeu d'esprit *and have no connection with the table.* (*V. and A. Museum*)

38 *Settee in the style of Kent, about 1735. Pinewood, carved, painted and gilded. (V. and A. Museum)*

of the period, although with a longer leg the curves are correspondingly less pronounced. Dining tables had flaps supported on swing legs, a continuation of the gate-leg principle; at first usually oval, they later tended to be rectangular in order that other flap tables could be placed at each end to form extensions. More immediately attractive are the folding gaming tables, on which much fine workmanship was expended and at which fortunes were won and lost at sessions of ombre and picquet. The majority are square, and of the four legs only one swings out to support the flap. This arrangement gives the table, when open, a lop-sided appearance. Better though more rare is a concealed concertina- or trellis-like mechanism whereby the table opens out into a square, all four legs remaining at the corners.

The habit of gambling was widespread, but the habit of tea-drinking soon became even more so. By the time of Queen Anne tea, which at first (soon after 1660) was regarded more as a curious tonic or medicine, was accepted as a pleasurable drink to be taken in society, as well as a useful antidote to the habit of excessive ale-quaffing and port-drinking indulged in by most gentlemen of the period. Imported by the East India Company, it was never cheap; dishonest servants were said to steal it and sell it on the equivalent of the black market. For this reason most eighteenth-century tea-caddies have locks, and the prudent housewife kept the key firmly attached to her person. Yet despite its cost its popularity swept like wildfire through all strata of society, and there were not wanting spoilsports and do-gooders who were only too ready to lecture the poor on the folly of spending their hard-earned wages on such a luxury. Even Dr Johnson (himself a noted tea-drinker) remarked that 'tea is a liquor not proper for the lower classes of the people, as it supplies no strength to labour, or relief to disease, but gratifies the taste without nourishing the body.' In this he was nearer the truth than he perhaps knew, for the kind of tea which working people could afford was so adulterated as to be little better than dust.

With the advent of tea as a social beverage came a whole range of objects connected with its making and drinking. Since it was so expensive it was made in the saloon or drawing room by the mistress of the house herself, the water being heated in a silver kettle suspended on a special stand over a small spirit lamp. The locked caddy would be brought in by a servant and ceremonially opened, the tea being then carefully measured out. Throughout the eighteenth and early nineteenth centuries much care and attention was lavished on the making of individual containers in silver, wood or glass, two or three usually being stored inside a silver or wooden caddy. The necessity for more than one container arose from the custom of blending different types of tea. The word caddy, though apparently not used until the end of the eighteenth century, derives from a Malaysian word *kati* indicating a weight approximating to one pound, and it was in small containers of such weight that the tea was originally imported. Before the establishment of 'caddy' the usual reference was to a tea-chest or tea-canister.

At first tea was drunk from little handle-less porcelain cups imported from China, whence came also the first tea pots in the familiar shapes that we recognise today. The absence of cup handles explains the contemporary phrase 'a dish of tay' (as they pronounced it then) and also emphasises the fact that people preferred their tea a good deal cooler than we normally do today.* It was also undoubtedly weaker, a fact partly dictated again by taste, partly by expense.

Once we in this country had discovered how to make soft-paste porcelain (as distinct from hard-paste, which is the true porcelain of China), the way was clear for the production by the Chelsea, Derby, Worcester, Bow and other famous manufactories of tea sets in a seemingly infinite variety of shapes, colours and patterns that continues to this day. Milk, it seems, was introduced into tea fairly early in the eighteenth century, and the popularity of cups either with or without handles ran parallel for many years from the 1740s on.

The social status of tea and the number of implements and accessories involved in tea-making quickly led to the introduction of special tea tables, kettle stands and other small pieces of furniture. The original form of the tea

---

*The phrase 'a dish of tay' may also have arisen from the alleged custom of pouring the tea into the deep saucers of the period and drinking it from them rather than direct from the cup.

39   *An interior and furniture both typical of the period around 1730. (V. and A. Museum)*

table as it appeared about 1700* was rectangular, but by the 1740s this had been superseded in popularity by the well-known tripod type which maintained its popularity for many years and is still one of the most sought-after forms of small eighteenth-century table, so much so that fakes and reproductions of it are legion. Claw-and-ball feet distinguish the finer and earlier specimens, and the tops are 'dished' – that is, carved out of the solid wood so as to leave a rim round the top. Any suggestion that this rim has been made separately and glued to the top should at once raise suspicions as to authenticity. As the century progressed it seems to have been customary for each person at a tea party to be supplied with his or her individual tripod table. By mid-century tripod tables were made with tiny balustraded galleries round the tops; at least some of these were probably intended for the display of porcelain or silver rather than for tea-taking.

* But a 1679 inventory at Ham lists 'one cedar tea table'.

During all this time scant attention was paid to designing special furniture for bedrooms and the other less important rooms in a house. When a piece became unfashionable it was simply pushed upstairs out of the way, and extreme contrast between the latest fashionable pieces in the main rooms and old-fashioned and even clumsily-made furniture in the secondary bedrooms was thought perfectly normal. Walnut went on being used for bedroom furniture in fashionable houses long after it had been banished from the reception rooms. But at least the chest-of-drawers had appeared shortly before the Restoration, about 1650, and by the 1720s had evolved into the elegant type sometimes known today as a 'bachelor's chest', probably because it has a folding top on which a valet might be expected to lay out his master's clothes for brushing. Later this top was replaced by a thin baize-topped shelf which slid into the body of the piece.

The two-stage tallboy, originally called the 'chest-upon-chest' and of Dutch origin, had also appeared; like the bureau-cabinet, it was in two separate parts, standing on bracket feet, and was surmounted by an overhanging cornice or sometimes by a pediment. Small kneehole dressing tables, like miniature desks, were made, as well as some examples standing on cabriole legs. In all such pieces the handles were in the loop form on shaped and solid back-plates.

Meanwhile one of the greatest advances in furniture-making at this time was quietly taking place, unseen and unrecognised. The handmade metal screw had arrived, and by about 1720 was being freely used in the construction of all types of furniture.

CHAPTER FOUR

Flights of Fancy –
Rococo, Chinoiserie and Gothic

IT MIGHT seem that the solemnities of the Palladian movement left no room for any kind of light relief in either architecture or furnishings. The English, however, are easily diverted, and by the 1740s many people were very ready to adopt a quite different style of decoration which contrasted oddly with the formalities of Palladianism. This new style we now call the Rococo, though it was not so described until the nineteenth century. The word itself derives from the French *rocaille* meaning literally 'rock-work', and indeed the style was born in France early in the eighteenth century as a form of decoration based on natural rock and shell formations. Quite soon, however, the original shapes became much more flowing and elaborate, having about them a jagged, spiky quality of line, whilst to rocks and shells were swiftly added a whole range of motifs inspired by animal and plant life.

In this country the new style was already beginning to take hold in the late 1730s, and English woodcarvers and plasterers learned much of the essential new techniques and changed approach to their art from immigrant Italian craftsmen, whose own plasterers or *stuccatori* were particularly skilled. For owing to the extreme variability and waywardness of its lines the Rococo style can only be carried out successfully in a medium that can be fairly easily moulded to the designer's wishes, such as wood or plaster (or even papier-mâché, as at Hartlebury Castle in Worcestershire). On the Continent this new, prickly style was often carried almost to excess. But there it had also to some extent an architectural function, whereas in England it remained almost exclusively a decorative style, confined to interior decoration, to the applied arts of furniture, ceramics and silver, and to engraved book illustration and trade cards. A greater contrast to the rigidly classical vocabulary of Palladian decoration (always, despite its great richness, somewhat forbidding and austere) could hardly be imagined.

Two other things distinguish the Rococo style. The first might almost be called a trademark, since it characterises the style more than anything else. It is the C-scroll motif, resembling an elaborate though shallower-than-normal version of the capital letter C which, facing in all directions and in all sizes, may

40   *Rococo chimneypiece of carved wood, mainly in the form of the C-scroll. About 1750.*
(V. and A. Museum)

be found in abundance on almost every piece of furniture and area whose decoration has been carried out in the Rococo style. Often the basic outline of a piece such as a mirror frame, or even of a large fitting such as a chimneypiece, will be found on close scrutiny to be almost entirely composed of variants of the C-scroll. The S-scroll is another, similar motif, though used to a lesser extent.

The second distinguishing feature of the Rococo is its deliberate cultivation of asymmetry – once again the very antithesis of the ordered and balanced designs of classicism. To test the truth of this, stand in front of a Rococo mirror frame and either draw an imaginary line down the centre or else blot out each half of the frame alternately by holding a hand in front of the eye. Almost certainly you will find that the two halves of the frame by no means match up; the details both of the outline and of the decoration of each half are likely to be widely different. Yet despite this the total effect will be one of balance and cohesion, and this is true of Rococo pieces in general.

In interior decoration the Rococo style is most often expressed in terms of plasterwork on walls and ceilings, where bunches of flowers, baskets of fruit and clumps of bulrushes (a favourite Rococo motif) replace the more formal designs of the classic manner, though often themselves contained within a still formal framework.

An important English (as opposed to immigrant) pioneer in the style was Matthew (or Matthias) Lock, a gifted carver who also published several books of Rococo designs. The first appeared in 1740 and was called *A New Drawing Book of Ornaments, Shields, Compartments, Masks etc.* In the Victoria and Albert Museum is a large mirror with console table to match, which was carved about 1743 by Lock and his assistants in what at first sight appears to be an imposing Palladian manner. However, closer inspection reveals a good deal of lively animal and plant life in the frame, which is surmounted at the very top by a rabbit's head – a slightly comic touch which, one feels, would have appealed to William Kent's sense of humour, though there is no evidence that he ever saw the mirror. It is a piece which illustrates very well the transition stage from formal Palladianism to the relaxed and cheerful Rococo.

In addition to Lock, one of the principal English designers to express the spirit of the Rococo positively was Thomas Johnson, himself also a carver. He published in 1755 an influential book of engraved plates entitled *Twelve Girandoles* (mis-spelt 'Gerandoles' on the original title-page). In no other piece is the essence of the Rococo so well distilled as in the girandole, perhaps because it is almost wholly decorative; the designer hardly needed to consider its functional aspect at all and could give full rein to his skill and imagination. The girandole is simply an ornamental wall-light, having one or more candle branches and often also incorporating a mirror. Johnson's book of designs confirmed the fashion for the girandole as a kind of miniature scene in carved and gilded wood – a deer hunt, a wind- or water-mill, or one of Aesop's fables – with the actual candle-holders as far as possible masquerading as naturalistic tree or shrub branches. The finished article never quite approaches the delicate cake-icing effect of the various designs in Johnson's book, but it often comes quite close. The same is true of mirror frames, which also lent themselves well to the Rococo style. Moreover the unpleasant effect of the join between the two plates of glass, which had always tended to spoil the full effect of the large Palladian mirrors, could now be avoided; the flowing nature of the Rococo lines made it possible to create frames in which all joints and joins between plates were effectively concealed by carved foliage and similar devices.

Other pieces which were especially singled out for Rococo treatment were wall-brackets, on which were stood pieces of porcelain, and torchères or candlestands. (The continued use of French words such as girandole and torchère illustrates the strong French influence which runs right through the Rococo style, itself then known in this country as 'the French taste'.) On such items will be found another very common form of Rococo decoration – a jagged fringe resembling icicles or stalactites, while the sinuous form of the dolphin seems to have had a special fascination for the carvers of torchères.

The essentially Rococo qualities of asymmetrical design and florid carving were obviously less suited to functional furniture such as chairs and tables. Yet even in these pieces tentative attempts had been made to express the new spirit during the 1740s. All the experiments and new ideas were summed up, and the way pointed forward for further developments, in a single book of designs published in 1754 under the now famous title of *The Gentleman and Cabinet-Maker's Director*. The designs were those of Thomas Chippendale, and basically they constituted a trade catalogue showing the kind of furniture that Chippendale could supply to his customers.

There are probably more popular misconceptions about Chippendale than about any other notable figure in English furniture history, with the possible exception of Hepplewhite and Sheraton. He was born in 1718 at Otley in Yorkshire; beyond this we know little about his early life, but we do know that by 1750 he had a cabinet-making business in Long Acre, London, and that he was successful enough to be able to move in 1753 to premises in St Martin's Lane, at that time a fashionable centre for cabinet-makers. He also acquired some influential patrons, a number of whom subscribed to the publication of the *Director* (as his book is usually called). Despite this he seems never to have supplied furniture to George III, whose official cabinet-makers were William Vile and John Cobb, Chippendale's neighbours in St Martin's Lane. His original workshop there (later burnt out in a fire) cannot have been large, for he seems to have employed only 22 workmen, a comparatively small number for a flourishing cabinet-making business of the period – which Chippendale's undoubtedly was. He died in 1779.

He describes himself on the title-page of the *Director* as 'Thomas Chippen-

41 *Design from Thomas Johnson's*
Twelve Girandoles, *1755. A girandole in*
the V. and A. Museum is based on this design

42 *Torchère or candlestand of carved and*
stained pinewood, about 1750. (V. and A.
Museum)

dale, Cabinet-Maker and Upholsterer'. (An alternative version of the word upholsterer at this period is upholder.) For an explanation of this apparently curious juxtaposition of trades we may turn to a book of 1747 entitled *The London Tradesman*, in which the author is supposedly building and fitting up a house:

I have just finished my house, and must now think of furnishing it with fashionable furniture. The Upholder is chief agent in this case: he is the man upon whose judgement I rely in the choice of goods; and I suppose he has not only judgement in the materials, but taste in the fashions, and skill in the workmanship. This tradesman's genius must be universal in every branch of furniture, though his proper craft is to fit up beds, window-curtains, hangings, and to cover chairs that have stuffed bottoms. . . . He employs journeymen in his own proper calling, cabinet-makers, glass-grinders, looking-glass frame-carvers, carvers for chairs, testers, and posts of beds, the woollen-draper, the mercer, the linen-draper, several species of smiths, and a vast many tradesmen of the other mechanic branches.

This passage shows, first, that the upholsterer of the period acted as a kind of general co-ordinating agent and interior design consultant. Chippendale was by no means alone among his contemporaries in combining the trades of upholsterer and cabinet-maker; such a combination made good economic sense, for, as the author of *The London Tradesman* remarks, 'A master cabinet-maker is a very profitable trade; especially if he works for and serves the quality himself; but if he must serve them through the channel of the upholder, his profits are not very considerable.'

Secondly, the passage illustrates the extent to which the various trades had fragmented into highly specialised compartments, each jealously guarding its own particular skills. Such specialisation is not, as we might think, a product of the twentieth century. To the list given above may be usefully added frame-makers (as distinct from frame-carvers), screen-makers, and gilders, who again divided themselves up by the different types of surfaces on which they worked, such as wood or metal.

In eighteenth-century France there was a period when the regulations of their trade guild compelled the master cabinet-makers of that country to stamp their work with their names. No such rules applied in England, and very few cabinet-makers regularly marked their own work. Some stuck paper trade labels inside drawers or onto the backs of larger pieces of furniture, but naturally not many of these labels have survived. Chippendale neither marked his pieces nor used trade labels; some existing letters, bills and household accounts for large houses such as Harewood House and Nostell Priory are the only proof of furniture having actually come from his workshop. As for the man himself, once firmly established in business he became primarily a director of his firm and a supplier of fashionable furniture, and most probably never touched a piece of wood from one month's end to another.

So it must be clearly understood that when a piece of eighteenth-century furniture is described as 'Chippendale', ninety-nine times out of a hundred what is really meant is that it is of the Chippendale period (about 1750 to 1780) and in the Chippendale style. Only in the hundredth case is the piece likely to have come from Chippendale's actual workshop. The word is misleading (sometimes, perhaps, deliberately so) and whenever possible should be qualified to 'Chippendale-style' or 'Chippendale-type'.

The real importance of Chippendale, both in his own day and in ours, lies in his designs. The publication of engraved plates of designs for furniture and fittings, 'pattern books' as they are called (such as Johnson's *Twelve Girandoles*), was an increasingly important element in eighteenth-century furniture production from the 1740s on. But of all the many collections that were published, Chippendale's was and has remained the most popular, the most influential and the most comprehensive. Moreover it was the first to be devoted solely to furniture, and in it are summarised all those elements of style that are so loosely called 'Chippendale', together with all the attempts that had been made up to that time to express the light-hearted, almost frivolous spirit of the Rococo in terms of functional furniture. In addition, the immediate and lasting popularity of the *Director* ensured that Rococo-inspired furniture became fashionable throughout the whole country. A second edition followed as early as 1755, and a third in 1762, though by that time the omission of certain plates from the edition and the inclusion of a number of entirely new ones reflected various minor changes in taste.

The general appearance of sober-looking Chippendale-style furniture in mahogany is well known. What is perhaps less well known is the fact that a large number of the original designs in the *Director* display far more carved Rococo decoration, some of it of great flamboyance, than most actual pieces made under the influence of those designs. Even in his own day Chippendale was accused of expecting too much from craftsmen, an accusation which he shrugged off in the following passage: 'Upon the whole, I have here [in the *Director*] given no design but what may be executed with advantage by the hands of a skilful workman, though some of the profession have been diligent enough to represent them . . . as so many specious drawings, impossible to be worked off by any mechanic whatsoever. I will not scruple to attribute this to malice, ignorance and inability.'

At the same time he was well aware that to many people the amount of ornamental carving he showed in his designs would appear excessive, and he expressly states more than once that much of it may be omitted at will (for example, 'A skilful workman may also lessen the carving, without any prejudice to the design', or, 'Part of the carving may be left out, if desired'). Much of it, indeed, was, and this is why so many pieces which are in Chippendale's manner are generally so very much simpler than his designs. In addition many craftsmen, especially those in provincial centres and country districts, while gladly adapting the designs in the *Director* to their own needs or those of their patrons, were notably reluctant to abandon certain traditional features, in particular the claw-and-ball foot; hence this is quite often found on chairs which in other respects are of the new design, though also often retaining the unfashionable stretcher.

The general chair pattern, which had been making tentative headway for some years and on which Chippendale set the final seal of approval in the first edition of the *Director*, was marked by square rather than rounded seats and backs, a cupid's-bow outline for the cresting rail, and a central splat of carved openwork. The back uprights tended to splay slightly outwards near the top. The Rococo-style chairs in Chippendale's designs almost all have the cabriole leg, but in fact a plain straight leg without a foot was becoming popular in all except the most highly fashionable models. For the feet of his own chairs Chippendale turned finally away from claw-and-ball and instead promoted other types more specifically Rococo in feeling and appearance; above all he favoured a curl- or scroll-foot whose origins were French. His armchairs too are specifically designated as 'French chairs' in the *Director*, probably because upholstered armchairs were more common at that time in France than in England. (They were all, of course, stuffed, not sprung; the first English patent for sprung upholstery is dated 1828.) But there is in any case considerable French influence on Chippendale's designs (a further reflection of French influence on the Rococo in general), and we know that he visited Paris in 1768. He even imported chairs from France, for in 1769 there was an embarrassing little matter of a fine by the Customs and Excise for under-declaring the value of 60 French chair frames, which he presumably intended to finish in his workshop. (However, the importing of French furniture was by no means rare at that period.) Such fashionable chairs were very often gilded. A type which was not was the 'ribband-back', in which the back splat is carved to represent a band of knotted ribbon. Although Chippendale probably got the idea from a French source he was justifiably proud of his own designs, of which he gave three in the *Director*, describing them without any trace of false modesty as 'the best I have ever seen (or perhaps have ever been made)'.

It should not be assumed that in his evident enthusiasm for the Rococo style Chippendale abandoned all tradition and decorum. Library furniture, for instance, tended to be always more sober and conservative than other pieces, as befitting the solemnities of such apartments. The provision of a library had become an increasingly important part of house planning since 1660, but more especially since the combined influences of the Grand Tour and Palladianism had prompted an interest in classical learning (the converse also being true, though perhaps to a lesser extent). Even for those landowners who had little or no interest in education a private library, with its shelves of volumes bound in leather and often stamped with the family crest, was something of a status symbol. In such temples of learning even the doors of adjoining rooms and closets were disguised as shelves, complete with rows of dummy book-backs. Thus it is not surprising that considerable space in the *Director* is occupied by designs for library desks, tables and bookcases, notable examples of which were installed by Chippendale at Nostell Priory in Yorkshire. Although heavier in appearance, the designs are enlivened by a judicious use of Rococo-inspired carving. However, even Chippendale was not ready to abandon the traditionally architectural outlines of large bookcases and bureaux, though the harsh angles of the typical Palladian broken pediment were now often softened

43 *Designs for 'ribband-back' chairs, from Chippendale's* Director, *3 ed., 1762*

44 *Designs for Chinese chairs, from the* Director, *1 ed., 1754. A prospective buyer could choose whichever half of a particular design he preferred*

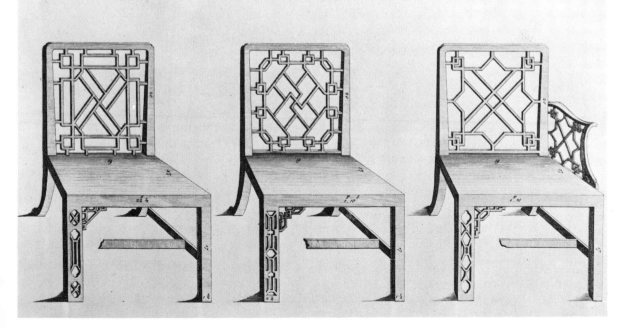

into the beautiful flowing shape known as a 'swan's neck' pediment. The so-called 'cockfighting' chair of the period is in reality intended for library use, having a small desk fixed to the back so that the reader, turning himself round, can use the chair as a stool and the incurving rail of the back as elbow supports. The typical library desk takes the familiar form of two pedestals containing drawers and with a central open space beneath the desk-top; Chippendale's finest essay in this field is the desk made originally for Harewood House but now at Temple Newsam House near Leeds.

Commode is a much misused and misunderstood term. In fact it is simply French for a low chest containing two or three drawers, and it is unfortunate that during the nineteenth century the word became attached in this country to imitation chests, cupboards, etc. that concealed chamber pots. French commodes, in the original sense of the word, range from those designed for bedroom use to those which are almost entirely ornamental and intended to stand in state apartments and reception salons. Examples of the last-named type began to be produced in France during the seventeenth century and reached their zenith in the eighteenth. They are distinguished by (1) the large amount

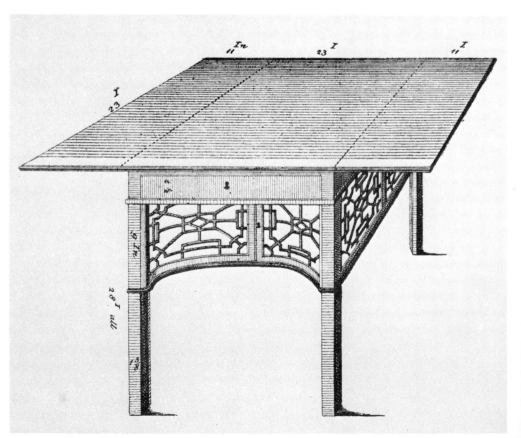

45 *Design for a breakfast table, from the* Director, *3 ed., 1762*

of exquisite marquetry they bear; (2) the 'bombé' front, which swells out like the wind-filled sails of a fine yacht; (3) the obligatory top of marble or scagliola whose front edge is often of cupid's bow or serpentine shape; (4) the numerous applied mounts of gilded bronze. This gilt bronze is known in England by the rather pretentious word 'ormolu', from the two French words *or moulu*, meaning literally ground-up gold. In fact the French themselves instead use the far more logical and truthful phrase *bronze doré*.

Commodes proper began to appear in fashionable English drawing rooms and salons about 1740, but the English-made commode is on the whole a much more restrained affair than the French, with a good deal less ornamentation, and English craftsmen tended not to make much use of the bombé front. Distinction was made between the French commode, which in this country meant the ornamental type, and the dressing commode which was plainer and intended for bedroom use – in fact, a true chest-of-drawers, though often embellished with serpentine front and metal mounts. The ornamental commode could by this time take the form of a cupboard as a change from the original conception with drawers. (It is perhaps worth mentioning that furniture purists refer to

46   *Breakfast table based on the preceding design. It is said that food was placed inside the latticed compartment, to keep it safe from household pets. (V. and A. Museum)*

the ornamental commode as a '*com*mode', stressing the first syllable, and to the humble but necessary night stool as a 'com*mode*.)' The drawer handles of the period are of the loop type, though the plates are now pierced in a fret-work style.

About 1750 mahogany began at last to enter the bedroom, where (as the *Director* shows) the focal point of decorative interest was now the elaborately carved tester head and carved bed pillars, once again emerging from the drap-eries that had swathed them closely for the past half-century. Chippendale also gives designs for chests and cupboards for clothes, some wildly extravagant ideas for ladies' dressing tables, and – more interestingly – some of the earliest printed designs for gentlemen's toilet requisites including 'A bason stand & glass' and 'A shaving table', both complete with basin, swing mirror and drawers; in addition the shaving table has a folding top which can be closed to conceal the basin and its surrounding small compartments.

So far we have been considering Chippendale's work in the context of Rococo art. But there is more to Chippendale than the Rococo, and more to the Rococo than the spiky, naturalistic style. We have already noted the post-Restoration upsurge of interest in things Oriental, as expressed in such forms as the craze for lacquered furniture, the adoption of tea, the popularity of the claw-and-ball foot. During the eighteenth century, and concurrently with the Rococo, this previously rather diffuse and vague enthusiasm for the Far East in general suddenly crystallised into a wildly extravagant vogue for a Chinese style, or Chinoiserie as it is often called, which reached its peak during the years 1745–55. Dragons, mandarins, pagodas, bells – all the stock decorative devices that Westerners who have never been to China associate with that country (or at least used to do), now began to be used freely as an ornamental vocabulary in their own right. But they seldom appear on their own, for more often than not they are inextricably mingled with the naturalism and the C-scrolls of the Rococo style itself. Indeed, the appeal of the Chinese taste at this particular time owed much of its strength precisely to the fact that its theme of the exotic and the picturesque fitted in so well with the basic underlying themes of the Rococo proper. Nor was it entirely coincidental that things like dragons and pagodas lent themselves particularly well to the woodcarving and plasterwork that are such a feature of Rococo decoration.

Once again ideas were spread abroad by means of the published pattern books; Lock's *A New Book of Ornaments* (1752) was the first in which Chinese motifs played an important decorative part in designs for mirror frames, girandoles and the like. And once again Chippendale's *Director* was probably the most influential of all the pattern books in propagating a style, in this case the Chinese. Pieces of furniture in the style form an important part of his book and show us another facet of his genius. His 'Nine designs of chairs after the Chinese manner' introduce us at once to that feature which is common in one way or another to almost all Chinese-style furniture – a sharply angular lattice or trellis pattern, of which there are seemingly endless varieties. In Chippendale's designs this lattice forms an openwork infilling of the chair back, replacing the traditional central splat; the chair legs, which are straight, square and without feet, are either pierced in the same style, or else the lattice pattern is shallowly carved on their surface, forming what is known as a blind fret frieze. The same frieze (though seldom in exactly the same pattern) may be found somewhere on almost any Chinese-style chair, couch, table or cabinet, as may also the openwork lattice. Chippendale's chairs in this style, as shown in the *Director*, are notably square and angular in outline as compared with the flowing and serpentine shapes of his Rococo designs, though by no means all existing examples are as uncompromisingly rigid-looking as his. Chinese lattice shapes and patterns were also widely used for the glazing bars on bureaux-bookcases, and there are many extant examples of this.

Some chairs in the Chinese taste will be found to have 'cluster column' legs, each one of which looks like four vertical rods joined together centrally like the leaves of a four-leaf clover. Perhaps the original idea was to suggest a

47 *Claydon House, Buckinghamshire. About 1755–1775. The Chinese tea pavilion, entirely carved from wood*

bundle of bamboo. Unlike his fashionable Rococo chairs, Chippendale does prescribe stretchers for his Chinese ones. Most chairs in the style (in fact, most Chinoiserie pieces) sport little carved bells, and somewhere there is usually to be found a suggestion, faint or positive, of pagodas – even if it is only in the fact that the cresting rail suddenly rises up to an angular peak in the middle.

The bulk of the Chinese designs in the *Director* are for cabinets and similar pieces, some of them extravagantly carved, though of one especially elaborate example Chippendale – as though to forestall criticism – states defiantly: 'This design I have executed with great satisfaction to the purchaser.' In the Victoria and Albert Museum is a small mahogany breakfast table, rectangular with two drop leaves, a shallow drawer and a compartment underneath enclosed by latticework; this corresponds to one of two designs in the *Director* for such pieces, for which there was an increasing demand as the custom of taking breakfast privately in one's bedroom became more widespread. But in fact there exist comparatively few Chinoiserie pieces which are at all closely based on the designs in the *Director*, and what was formerly supposed to be Chippendale's own most famous essay in the style is now thought to be the work of his able contemporary John Linnell. This is a set of bedroom furniture made for the Duke of Beaufort and including a magnificent bed like a small Chinese temple without walls (also now in the Victoria and Albert Museum).

On the other hand a good deal of mid-eighteenth-century Chinoiserie furniture has survived, testifying to the extreme popularity of the style. However, it was not without its critics, one of whom writing in 1753 complained bitterly that, 'Chairs, tables, chimneypieces, frames for looking-glasses, and even our most vulgar utensils, are all reduced to this new-fangled standard: and without doors, so universally has it spread that every gate to a cow-yard is in Ts and Zs [a reference to the trellis pattern], and every hovel for cows has bells hanging at the corners.'

The outdoor spread of the fashion was perhaps not quite so universal as this extract suggests, being mostly confined to ornamental garden pavilions and tea-houses on pagoda-like lines. Of such buildings, however, there was certainly no lack. The first to appear was very probably a little tea pavilion in the grounds of Shugborough in Staffordshire, but the best-known is considerably larger – the famous Pagoda in Kew Gardens, built in 1762 to the design of the architect Sir William Chambers (though there was an earlier pagoda – now destroyed – also at Shugborough). This was a piece of youthful exuberance on the part of Chambers, who came to regret it, together with what he himself later called the 'extravagant fancies that daily appear under the name of Chinese'. He had good reason to be critical, for he alone amongst the horde of Chinoiserie designers had, in his youth, actually visited China (on trade voyages with the Swedish East India Company), had noted carefully many details of national architecture and decoration there, and after returning to Europe had published in 1757 a book of plates entitled *Designs for Chinese Buildings, Furniture, Dresses Etc*. Thus

48 *Detail of the central carving inside the tea pavilion at Claydon. The gestures may be variously interpreted*

the more the style was misinterpreted and abused by his contemporaries, the more Chambers came heartily to dislike it and to wish that he had never built the Pagoda. The casual attitude towards Chinoiserie that Chambers most despised is neatly summed up by a character in a novel of 1796 (*Angelina*, by Mary Robinson), who, on expressing his intention to build a pagoda in the grounds of his mansion, adds: 'Besides, a pagoda will be of some use, one can breed pigeons; – and I like that sort of building – it looks so lively with the gilt bells and things, painted in different colours.'

No eighteenth-century English house has a Chinese exterior, but very many have details of interior decoration springing from the current fashion; these range from hand-painted wallpaper with Chinese motifs to whole rooms conceived in the Chinese style, such as the re-created dressing room at Saltram House (Devonshire). The most complete of such inspirations is the Chinese room at Claydon House (Buckinghamshire), where even the overdoors are elaborately-carved temple façades, and where the main feature is a tea pavilion, a room-within-a-room, exquisitely carved throughout in wood and hung all over with the inevitable tiny carved bells.

The craze for Chinoiserie at its most extreme died out during the 1760s, after a comparatively brief flowering of which Claydon (begun in 1768) provides both the finest and the latest eighteenth-century example of importance. (It enjoyed a short revival during the Regency period, which will be discussed in a later chapter.) The craze for Gothic, on the other hand, though beginning in earnest at about the same time, actually lasted much longer and was prolonged well on into the Victorian era.

Elements of Gothic – the architectural style of the Middle Ages – had been used fitfully by Wren, Hawksmoor, Vanbrugh, and even William Kent. Indeed 'Kentian Gothic', as it might be called, was sufficiently popular by 1742 for a book to appear with the lengthy and intimidating title, *Gothic Architecture, Improved by Rules and Proportions, in many Grand Designs of Columns, Doors, Windows . . . Temples, and Pavilions etc.* This had been put together by Batty Langley, a prolific writer on architecture and related subjects as well as a practising architect and builder. But the Gothic of Kent and Langley was a flimsy affair – merely a gimcrack façade, one feels, for solid Palladian principles lurking behind it. An entirely new and much more important angle on the style can be traced to one man and one house – Horace Walpole and Strawberry Hill, Twickenham. Horace (1717–1797), a son of the powerful politician Sir Robert Walpole and himself later Earl of Orford, bought Strawberry Hill in the early 1740s; it was then a modest early Georgian building situated in an up-and-coming country district within easy travelling distance of London. A year or two later he had conceived the idea of altering the appearance of the house, both inside and out, so as to give it a vaguely medieval appearance that would be in tune with his own interests in the historical, literary and romantic past. With the help and advice of some enthusiastic friends, and with a professional architect-cum-builder named Robinson on hand to carry out the ideas, Horace Walpole succeeded over a period of 30 years in completely changing the character and appearance of Strawberry Hill. The original modest house changed gradually into a 'venerable pile' complete with battlements, pseudo-medieval windows and doorways with pointed arches, buttresses, and a great round tower. But the really significant feature of the house's appearance was the studied irregularity of its western façade, which gave – as it was intended to do – the impression of having evolved haphazardly, an impression which so many genuine medieval buildings do in fact give. This, the complete antithesis of planned Palladianism, was to have far-reaching effects.

At Strawberry Hill conscious medievalism is everywhere expressed in a riot of what Horace himself (though speaking here specifically of his library) called 'arches and pinnacles and pierced columns'; there is a chimneypiece based on the tomb of Archbishop Wareham in Canterbury cathedral, an imitation fan-vaulted ceiling in the Gallery that instantly reminds us of St George's chapel, Windsor, Henry VII's chapel in Westminster Abbey or King's College chapel, Cambridge, all rolled into one, another ceiling copied from the Chapter House in York Minster, and many other pseudo-medieval extravaganzas. But it is all good fun, and in spirit (even to some extent in execution) is not far removed from that of the Rococo. Above all, it is neither solemn nor dull.

49 *Strawberry Hill, Twickenham. Developed by Horace Walpole from 1748 onwards. His earliest work is the section on the right, up to the first buttress of the gallery range*

50   *Strawberry Hill. The Gothic staircase, in fact designed by Walpole's friend Richard Bentley*

Walpole's contemporaries loved it, and soon crowds of elegant sightseers were flocking daily to Strawberry Hill – so many, in fact, that guided tours (conducted by the owner) had to be restricted to one per day. It can safely be said that many an English house was 'Gothicised', in part or in whole, during the latter half of the eighteenth century as a direct result of Horace Walpole's transformation of Strawberry Hill.

Despite the widespread popularity and influence of Strawberry Hill, however, no completely new house showing that influence appeared until 1785, when the professional architect James Wyatt (1746–1813) created Lee Priory (Kent) for one of Walpole's own friends. Horace himself generously called it 'a child of Strawberry, and prettier than the parent'. It was in fact an even more successful essay in the mock-medieval than Strawberry, firstly because Wyatt, building from the ground up and not merely altering an already existing house, was able to carry out completely that impression of haphazard medieval growth which at Strawberry Hill is confined mainly to the west front; secondly, because his knowledge and correct application of medieval decoration was more complete than Walpole's. This, however, unfortunately did not prevent him from carrying out some rather drastic 'restorations' in a number of churches and cathedrals, where his ill-advised measures earned him the name, among his critics, of 'Wyatt the Destroyer'.

Fittingly therefore it was Wyatt who was called upon to build that extraordinary mansion Fonthill Abbey which, though no longer standing, has become the epitome of the enthusiasm for Gothic. The house began as the brain-child of the eccentric millionaire William Beckford, who in 1796 conceived the very Gothic idea of having a romantic 'ruined convent' specially built on his huge Wiltshire estate, and asked Wyatt to take on the work. During the following years the ideas and the convent both grew, until in 1807 Beckford decided to demolish the perfectly sound Palladian family mansion in which he had been living elsewhere on the estate, and to go and live permanently in the Abbey, as it was now to be called. This had become a complete building, in appearance part castle, part cathedral; the plan was cross-shaped, and the undeniably dramatic cluster of ancient-looking buildings centred round an enormous octagonal tower that soared over 276 feet into the air and was partly modelled on the lantern tower of Ely cathedral, while being a good deal less secure, as will shortly be appreciated.

Inside, Fonthill was no less impressive, with a huge Octagon Hall 120 feet high beneath the central lantern, and wings some 400 feet long and 25 feet wide. But it was also highly inconvenient. From kitchen to dining room measured 250 yards, while the 18 bedrooms were small, badly-lit and ill-ventilated, and some involved a steep climb of 80 feet. The various inconveniences at last became too much even for the intrepid Beckford, and in 1822 he sold the house and moved to Bath. Six years later the central tower of Fonthill suddenly collapsed, and though the rest of the house was undamaged it was eventually

51   *The drawing room at Arbury Hall, Warwickshire. This Tudor home was partly Gothicised about 1750 by Sanderson Miller, an enthusiastic amateur whose approach to Gothic was more frivolous than that of Walpole (who disliked him)*

abandoned and allowed to fall into genuine ruin. Today only fragments of it remain.

Three things had contributed to the collapse. First, the foundations had never been properly completed, the money assigned for this essential work having found its way into various people's pockets. Second, the tower, for all its apparent solidity, had consisted merely of a timber framework with a thin cladding of stone. Third, and perhaps most important of all, Wyatt himself was a constitutionally lazy man; had he given greater personal attention to the work, no doubt the foundations would have been laid according to the plans. But even the energetic Beckford had not been able to cure the architect of his human failings. In the words of a contemporary, 'Beckford is much dissatisfied with Wyatt, who perpetually disappoints him. He said if Wyatt can get near a big fire and have a bottle by him, he cares for nothing else.'

In fact Fonthill was probably one of the largest examples of a folly ever to be built in this country. A folly, as a building, is simply an architectural oddity or extravaganza, and as such was particularly well suited to the Gothic taste of the eighteenth century. Hence sham castles and ready-made ruins sprang up apace all over England, often so convincing in appearance as to make the uninitiated even today suppose that here is a genuine piece of really ancient building. But it is important to recognise that Gothic is as much a literary movement as an architectural one; the two are closely linked, and they developed together. Gothic novels of the period deal at length with the occult, the supernatural and the romantic, and it is no coincidence that both Walpole and Beckford had written such novels – *The Castle of Otranto* and *Vathek* respectively. At Fonthill much of the house was deliberately dimly-lit, the servants were dressed as monks, and perfumed coal burned in the grates; strange rites (it was rumoured) were celebrated, culminating in the infamous Black Mass. However, this was exceptional; few other people (except perhaps the members of Sir Francis Dashwood's Hellfire Club) were prepared to take their enthusiasm for Gothic to such lengths. When an eighteenth-century gentleman named Mr Bateman, who lived in Old Windsor, converted his house inside to look like a monastery and named two of the bedrooms 'the monkish apartments', he himself had of course no intention of renouncing the world and embracing a 'monkish' way of life.* It is essential to recognise that Strawberry Hill Gothic is primarily a light-hearted decorative style (and is thus akin to the Rococo proper), only superficially linked with the medieval architectural styles from which it allegedly derives. The relevance of this fact will be seen even more clearly when we come to discuss the Victorian version of Gothic. In the light of it, the sham ruins, mock battlements, imitation cloisters, false arrow-slits and all the rest of the architectural paraphernalia of eighteenth-century 'Gothick' are seen correctly in their wider context.

From Strawberry Hill onwards, 'Gothick' furniture was concocted to fit in with Gothic interiors. Needless to say it bore little or no relation to genuine medieval furniture but was simply a re-interpretation in Gothic terms of current eighteenth-century designs; even Chippendale included a few Gothic designs in his *Director*. The Gothic influence is always recognisable by the use of the pointed arch device; this can appear as a chair back infilling or as the back outline itself, as a blind fret frieze on a table, as the outline of a china cabinet or bookcase, and so on. A common variation on the simple pointed arch is the ogee arch, thus:

* *The autobiography and correspondence of Mary Granville, Mrs Delany*, vol. I, second series, 1862. Mrs Delany (a personal friend of George III and his family) states that in fact the house had been converted 'from the Indian to the Gothic'.

As in the Chinese style, the legs of Gothic tables, chairs and cabinets go straight down to the ground without feet. But Gothic chairs in particular sometimes show two features which might cause one to confuse them with Chinoiserie. In the first place they often bear fret carving, either blind or pierced, in trellis-like patterns similar to the Chinese. In the second, they may have the same kind of cluster column legs, though here the inspiration is obviously not bundles of bamboo but more probably the shafts of stone and Purbeck marble which form the pillars in some medieval churches and cathedrals, for example Salisbury. Such slight complications apart, it is generally not difficult to recognise a piece of eighteenth- or early nineteenth-century Gothic furniture, nor to differentiate it from the much heavier style which characterises Victorian Gothic pieces.

CHAPTER FIVE

The Adam Revolution

Revolution is a strong word, but not too strong to describe the tremendous impact made by the architect Robert Adam on the building and interiors (especially the latter) of later eighteenth-century English houses. Moreover, what is now universally known as the Adam style has become so familiar that many people can recognise it immediately, almost instinctively, though perhaps without knowing exactly why.

Robert Adam was born in 1728, the second son of William Adam of Kirk-caldy near Edinburgh, a Scottish Palladian architect of ability and some repute. As a young man, Robert made the visit to Italy which by now was expected of every aspiring young artist, and on his return in 1758 set up in architectural practice in London, where he was joined by his younger brothers James and, later, William and by two of his sisters; they formed a close-knit and affectionate family. We tend to forget the part played by James Adam in the formation and propagation of the Adam style, but his talents as an architect were considerable.

The Adam brothers set out consciously and deliberately to replace the rigid Palladianism of the past 30-odd years with something sufficiently new and startling to become quickly fashionable, yet having more substance than the frivolities of the Rococo. They got off to a good start, partly through having influential friends in high places including the powerful politician Lord Bute, a fellow Scot, and their commissions increased so rapidly that by the mid-1760s they were engaged on work at a dozen or more important houses scattered throughout the country from London to Yorkshire.

The new style is less obvious from the outside. By the time Robert Adam started out on his career, the building or remodelling of many important country houses in the once-fashionable Palladian manner was either well under way or had already been completed; thus all too often he was called in to complete work already begun under other architects, and only very rarely got the opportunity to build an entirely new house. When he did, the commissions were mostly comparatively small and the result (such as Mersham-le-Hatch, Kent) correspondingly modest. The one really large house he built, Luton Hoo

53 *Syon House, Brentford, London. Here in Adam's Entrance Hall the floor tiles mirror the ceiling design. The screen formed by a beam supported on columns is another favourite Adam device*

Greek style was too stark to please everyone, and a fierce 'battle of the styles' arose as to the relative merits of Greek versus Roman architecture. Wise artists stood aside from this largely sterile battle of words, quietly absorbing the best from both styles, and the specific influence of Greek classicism on Adam is seen architecturally in such features as the Osterley portico, decoratively in the frequent use of such motifs as the anthemion (a stylised Greek version of the honeysuckle flower).

It will be noticed that many of Adam's most thoroughly classical apartments are entrance halls, where the intention was to overawe the visitor. (Dr Johnson, however, refused to be overawed at Kedleston: 'The pillars', he remarked characteristically, 'are very large and massy, they take up too much room, they were better away.') It is in the other rooms that we may expect to find the essence of the Adam style. For their interior decorations Inigo Jones and the Palladians had simply used the various columns, motifs and friezes that the Romans had used in their temples and important public buildings. Adam, on the other hand, recognised that Roman domestic interiors had actually been decorated in a much lighter, flowing style, in which painted decoration figured on an equal basis with mouldings and other applied work; he had been able to study this style for himself whilst in Italy, notably in the recently-begun (1738) excavations at Herculaneum, and his brother James later continued these researches at Pompeii where excavation did not begin until 1763. Other examples were to be found amid the ruins of the various palaces and public buildings that still existed at Rome.

In fairness we should note that Adam was not alone in appreciating that Roman interior decoration differed fundamentally from the Palladian view of it. To his criticism of Kent (quoted on p. 70), Horace Walpole adds significantly: 'Indeed I much question whether the Romans admitted regular architecture *within* their houses. At least the discoveries at Herculaneum testify that a light and fantastic architecture, of a very Indian air, made a common decoration of private apartments.'

The basic ingredients of this decoration are not really in any way 'Indian' but consist of all kinds of fantastic human and animal figures, garlands, scrolls and the like, executed in a thin, linear style and known as grotesques. In this usage the word was not intended to convey anything ugly or misshapen. 'By grotesque', writes Adam himself, 'is meant that beautiful light style of ornament used by the ancient Romans in the decoration of their palaces, baths and villas.' He further explains that the word comes from the Italian *grottesche* (grottoes), which was originally used during the Renaissance to refer to excavated buildings of classical Rome. (Perhaps 'grotto-esque' would be a more meaningful rendering in English.) These Roman-inspired grotesques appear in the decorative work of the Renaissance artists, especially that of Raphael and his school, whose work thus provided Adam with yet another fruitful source for his own decorative style.

Nevertheless, it should be noted that he did not abandon the traditional mouldings favoured by the Palladians, but continued to make use of them where he felt them to be appropriate, supplementing them with mouldings and friezes composed of newly-introduced motifs such as the Greek honeysuckle.

The grotesque style was not unknown in this country before Adam. There was considerable use of it during the Elizabethan period, when it was imbibed at second hand from the Italian Renaissance artists, but although found in plasterwork it was used far less in interior decoration than on artifacts such as silverware. However, it occasionally and surprisingly crops up in more severely classical settings – for example, in one of the rooms in Inigo Jones's Queen's House, and at Kensington Palace and Rousham House (Oxfordshire), both decorated by Kent who, like Adam, had evidently seen and imbibed something of the Roman interior style whilst in Italy.

In addition to the grotesques proper, Adam made use of long, flowing and curving lines which often break out into leafy fronds as they curl about; these are known as arabesques. Other favourite motifs are rams' heads, swags, urns, tripods, putti (cherubs), gryphons and winged sphinxes. (There are also some very curious animal hybrids such as the lions in the frieze round the Library at Kenwood, whose tails become luxuriant arabesques.) All these devices were mixed together as the occasion and setting demanded, reproduced in plaster, paint, wood or other materials, on walls or ceilings, resulting in the famous 'Adam style'. In fact the style is not of course peculiar to the Adam brothers but is the specifically British manifestation of the European-wide art movement of the period known as Neo-classicism. However, this term (which only means 'new-style classicism') need not detain us here, and the novice student of Adam's work will gain far more insight into its essential characteristics by looking at the panels of grotesques in the Osterley Eating Room than by reading books about Neo-classicism.

Robert Adam was under no illusion as to the importance of what he and his brother James had achieved, nor was he inhibited by any sense of false modesty. 'The massive entablature, the ponderous compartment ceiling, almost the only species of ornament formerly known in this country, are now universally exploded', he wrote proudly, if rather quaintly, 'and in their place we have adopted a beautiful variety of light mouldings, gracefully formed, delicately enriched, and arranged with propriety and skill. We have introduced a great diversity of ceilings, friezes and decorated pilasters, and have added grace and beauty to the whole by a mixture of grotesque, stucco and painted ornament.' He had recognised what Inigo Jones and the Palladians had not – that, to the ancient Romans, decoration was not a matter of rigid rules, but rather one of feeling for the sympathetic interpretation of those rules.

Thus the keynote of the new style was its lightness and delicacy, as opposed to the heavy touch of the Palladian school, though many of the basic ingredients

54   *Osterley. The Eating Room, showing the original furniture arranged as Adam intended, including the group of sideboard table and urns. The panels of grotesques are as entirely typical of Adam as the Rococo-style ceiling is not*

remained the same. The compartmented ceilings, the columns, pilasters, cornices and friezes are refined away until virtually nothing remains but delicate cobwebby plaster tracery on walls and ceilings, enhanced by a subtle use of pastel colours. (Adam's original designs show that his colours and colour contrasts were often a good deal stronger than we perhaps imagine, and this sometimes leads to argument and dissatisfaction when his work is restored today. Similar arguments surround newly-cleaned paintings in the National Gallery and elsewhere.) Indeed the thin, linear quality of Adam's decoration became so extreme as his career progressed that critics spoke scathingly of his 'gingerbread and sippetts of embroidery. . . . All the harlequinades of Adam that never let the eye repose for a moment' (Horace Walpole, who began by admiring Adam's work but later changed his mind about it), of his 'filigrane toy-work' (Sir William Chambers, who disliked Adam in any case), and of his 'puerile ornament' (Peacock, a lesser architect). The best house in which to study this gradual progression of his style is Osterley, for he was at work there, on and off, for almost 20 years, from 1761 onwards.

Not only was the style of decoration new – so were many of the materials and methods used. The Adam brothers, as a firm, were the first to become interested in early forms of mass-production and to make use of new industrial processes and materials then coming onto the market as a result of the Industrial Revolution; these included cast iron, composition metal, Coade stone (the secret of which is now lost) and papier-mâché (occasionally used earlier in the century, however), all of them being utilised at one time or another by the Adams. There was even a form of central heating at Kedleston, though nobody seems certain today exactly how this worked. When the architect Sir John Soane later remarked that, 'manufacturers of every kind felt . . . the electric power of this [Adam] revolution in art', he was not exaggerating. In fact it is true to say that over-reliance on mass-production was at least partly to blame for the decline in standards of workmanship and quality which mars too much of the brothers' later work.

One of Robert Adam's principal achievements was to attract to himself a team of loyal artists and craftsmen of the highest calibre, who carried out his designs for him. This team included, at one time or another, the plasterers Joseph Rose (uncle and nephew having the same name), the sculptors Joseph Wilton, Michael Spang and Thomas Carter, the painters Giovanni Battista Cipriani, Biagio Rebecca, Francesco Zuccarelli, Antonio Zucchi and Angelica Kauffmann. The last two (who later married; Angelica was also one of the two women founder members of the Royal Academy in 1768, the other being Mary Moser) were perhaps employed more consistently by Adam than any of the others, and they were kept very busy, for paintings – especially on ceilings – were an important part of his decorative schemes. In several of his dining rooms Adam provided a series of plaster wall frames, symmetrically arranged, which Zucchi had to fill with landscape paintings. These pictures were not then looked on as works of art in their own right, but simply as elements of the general decoration. It is therefore not surprising if they seem on the whole to be rather uninspired. Classical mythology formed the subject for most of Zucchi's other paintings and for those of Angelica Kauffmann, who was also a good portrait painter in her own right. Indeed it seems that the two of them kept a supply of ready-painted pictures on hand, from which Adam could select the ones most suited to the schemes that he was currently working on.

Work by the two Josephs Rose (who each complicated matters by having a son named Jonathan who assisted him) is to be found in most houses where Adam is known to have been involved in the decorations, though it is seldom possible to tell exactly which member of the family was involved in any one particular commission. The style of their workmanship is perhaps seen at its very best in the great clusters (known as trophies) of classical weapons and military accoutrements which, contained within panels and executed in high relief, lend an air of solemn distinction to the more formal apartments such as the Entrance Hall at Osterley and the Ante-Chamber at Syon.

Two other important craftsmen who were associated with Robert Adam in his work were the Birmingham metal-master Matthew Boulton and the famous potter Josiah Wedgwood. One of Boulton's specialities was a type of gilded metal that he himself had developed and of which Adam made extensive use on door-frames, chimneypieces and so on, especially at Syon and Osterley. Wedgwood (himself obviously strongly influenced by Adam's style) made plaques and panels in his celebrated blue-and-white jasperware which Adam both incorporated into his schemes and also occasionally imitated in plaster, as in the Music Room at Mellerstain (Berwickshire).

Adam's name is linked with that of Wedgwood in another respect also. The visitor to Osterley will find himself, at the end of that splendid range of state apartments, in a curious place called the Etruscan Dressing Room. This is indeed a dressing room, designed to supplement the bedroom next door, but the walls are somewhat sparsely decorated with grotesques (painted on canvas) which Adam claimed were 'imitated from the vases and urns of the Etruscans'. In fact, in spite of their predominantly black and russet colouring, these grotesques bear little relation to the kind of one-dimensional scenes to be found on the Greek Attic vases which Adam claimed had inspired him – though he, in common with everyone else at that time, made the mistake of believing the vases to be Etruscan in origin. Nevertheless 'Etruscan' pottery was then attracting a great deal of attention, so much so that Wedgwood named his new factory at Burslem 'Etruria' and by the late 1760s was producing a wide and highly popular range of wares decorated in the Greek style.

The Etruscan Room at Osterley therefore bears witness to a minor yet important offshoot of taste of the period; designs for it are dated 1775 and 1779, and that it was no mere flash in the pan is proved by the fact that Adam provided similar rooms for at least five other houses, though of them all Osterley alone survives. (His rival James Wyatt also designed Etruscan rooms, at Heaton Hall, Manchester, and Heveningham Hall, Norfolk, respectively, and these may still be seen.) The Osterley Etruscan Room may strike some visitors as cold and uninviting, especially as a dressing room. Horace Walpole certainly thought so. 'The last chamber . . . chills you', he writes, and continues bitingly, 'It would be a pretty waiting-room in a garden. I never saw such a profound tumble into the Bathos. It is like going out of a palace into a potter's field.'

The Adam 'revolution' took place mainly during the 1760s and early '70s, and the new style in interior decoration obviously required a new style of furniture to complement it. This was true no less of the various Etruscan rooms than of Adam's more conventional apartments. For the Etruscan Room at Osterley Adam provided a set of eight beechwood armchairs, painted with 'Etruscan' ornament in terracotta red and black on grey; the chairs are four-square and have cane seats intended to take squab cushions. Designed in 1776, they may well be among the earliest painted armchairs in existence. Certainly they seem more fitted to Walpole's 'waiting-room in a garden' than to a house, but the back splat is of interest, for its shape is obviously based on that of a Greek vase and illustrates Adam's ingenious use of antique forms in furniture, not merely as decoration but as actual structural members. Again, in the fine set of Eating Room chairs at Osterley the shape of that ancient Greek harp, the lyre, is introduced as the back splat, and the same motif is repeated in the backs of the Osterley Library chairs (though these seem to have been designed by John Linnell).

People today are sometimes disappointed to find that the back views of such beautiful chairs are very often completely plain, in contrast to the carved and/or other ornament which they may bear elsewhere on the frame. This is because at that period in all but the most private apartments chairs and other pieces of furniture were not scattered about the room in our modern fashion but were ranged round the walls unless actually in use; thus the backs were seldom seen, and the centre of the room was left empty so that the company could 'circulate'. This applied also to dining tables which often were not even kept in the dining room but in a passage or corridor outside (as at Osterley), and were only brought in when a meal was imminent. (Fashion in costume often dictates fashions in the other arts; thus it is also quite feasible that the voluminous skirts of the period, requiring as they did plenty of space in which to move, forced furniture to the walls.)

These conditions, which had prevailed since the sixteenth century, changed suddenly soon after 1800. A visitor to Osterley in 1810 writes: 'Tables, sofas and chairs were studiously *derangés* about the fire-places, and in the middle of the rooms, as if the family had just left them, although the house has not been inhabited for several years. Such is the modern fashion of placing furniture, carried to an extreme, as fashions are always, that the apartments of a fashionable house look like an upholsterer's or cabinet-maker's shop.'* And Jane Austen, in a typical tongue-in-cheek passage in *Persuasion*, speaks of various small tables and other articles of furniture scattered about the drawing-room 'to give the proper air of confusion'. Thus our ideas on arranging furniture are no older than the Regency (when, it may be noted, women's dress also became more manageable). However, there are signs that some house owners had never really taken to the parade-ground-like appearance of the main reception rooms, which may have been forced on them by designers (including Adam himself) in the name of fashion, and that they were only too glad to throw off such shackles and introduce a new note of comfortable informality.

Adam's chairs and tables are stylistically closely linked. Both have delicately tapered legs, round or square, ending in peg or spade feet, and being either

* L. Simond, *Journal of a tour and residence in Great Britain during the years 1810 and 1811*, vol. II, p. 285. 2 ed., 1817.

55 *Osterley. The State bed, with typical Adam chairs. The thin ceiling decoration and frieze of anthemion indicate Adam's later decorative style*

fluted or reeded. (Fluting consists of carved parallel concave grooves, whilst reeding presents a surface of parallel convex strips.) This decoration is also applied to the seat-rail (in chairs) and frieze (tables), while the ornament most common to both chairs and tables is the patera, a Greek device consisting of an oval or round decoration like a sunflower, which is carved, inlaid or painted on the piece, usually at the corners above the legs. It is worth noting that Adam's table legs are often extremely complicated in design, being formed from a variety of different shapes built up vertically one upon another.

Adam's early efforts in furniture designing were somewhat tentative, since before the 1760s he had, so far as we know, no practical experience in that field; it is therefore not surprising if, for example, some of his first pieces show definite signs of having been influenced by Kent. Others perhaps owe their inspiration to James Stuart, in particular to some furniture designs which he produced in 1757 or '58 for Lord Curzon. By the '70s, however, Adam was supplying pieces which are either unmistakably his own (as attested by original designs) or else produced under his direct influence and perhaps supervision. Notable amongst these are the elegant oval-backed armchairs with rounded seats, the backs themselves supported on two small uprights (sometimes in the shape of sphinxes), the arms supported on backward-sweeping uprights. These chairs are particularly associated with the various Tapestry Rooms which Adam created for four different patrons, and the idea for the first of these, at Croome Court, together probably with designs for its furniture, he seems to have obtained in 1763 via his patron Lord Coventry from the Gobelins tapestry manufactory in Paris. But if the original designs were French, there is no doubt that Adam very swiftly made them his own. The tapestries themselves were based on the designs of Boucher, and the chairs were similarly upholstered in tapestry to match. The Croome Court room is now in New York's Metropolitan Museum, but the Osterley and Newby Hall Tapestry Rooms still survive, with their furniture.

One of Adam's outstanding innovations was the design and grouping of the dining room sideboard with attendant free-standing urns on pedestals, one at each side of the sideboard itself (at this period still an ornamental table with a marble top). The group was sometimes completed by a large bath-like wine-cooler standing underneath the sideboard, and all the pieces in this group were designed as a single decorative entity. Adam believed that some of the most far-reaching political and social decisions of the time were made by gentlemen sitting over their port after meals (he may well have been right), and he therefore conceived his sideboard group in suitably grandiose terms to emphasise the solemn importance of the room. Today it may all look rather empty and pompous, especially the urns which seem to be totally useless until one discovers that they do in fact have various functions. Some are lined with lead and have little taps at the base; these contained water. Others did duty as knife boxes (cutlery at that time being stored upright) or wine bins. The pedestals on which they stand often had similar parts to play; some again were wine bins, others contained plate racks and tiny spirit lamps for warming the plates, or lead-lined tanks in which glasses and cutlery were rinsed by the butler as the meal progressed, in readiness for the next course. And some pedestals undoubtedly concealed the chamber pot which was kept at hand so that gentlemen's after-dinner drinking and conversation need not long be interrupted by mere calls of nature.

For all his insistence on the importance of the Eating Room, Adam designed no dining tables. These, as has already been shown, were still stored outside the room and only set up for meals; consequently they tended to be plain, with drop-leaves for easy storage. There are, however, flap dining tables in the Adam style, with the usual tapered legs, fluted or reeded friezes, etc., and these were still set together to produce one large table when necessary.

Nor, so far as is known, did Adam ever design more than three beds. Most important is the one at Osterley, a grand affair like a small temple, surmounted by a dome which was originally festooned with artificial flowers. (Horace Walpole found this especially shocking, exclaiming: 'What would Vitruvius think of a dome decorated by a milliner!') The woodwork (oak, beech and pine) is painted and gilded, and the whole thing is hung about with elaborate draperies whose colour is predominantly a soft green.

Adam reserved some of his finest strokes of imagination for his wall-furniture – mirrors, side-tables and commodes – and for semi-ornamental, semi-functional pieces such as pedestals and candlestands. The latter are often in the tripod form associated with the small portable altar or incense-burner of classical times, and bear a wealth of typical Adam ornament executed in carved and painted wood and gilt metal. Also notable, though all too often unnoticed, are the beautiful gilt metal lamps and hanging lanterns which Adam designed for such houses as Osterley and Syon.

Up to about 1770 the typical Adam commode was rectangular, but at the peak of his mature style he turned to a semicircular form, of which probably the finest examples are a pair at Osterley designed in 1773 for the Drawing Room there. They are entirely ornamental, having neither drawers nor cupboards, and each has a huge mirror (134 inches in length) above it to match. It was Adam's practice in such cases to bring the edge of the mirror glass right down to join the back edge of commode or table, giving the effect of a single unit. By this time it was possible to obtain mirror glass in sufficiently large sheets to avoid the unsightly business of having two plates of unequal size, but at first such very large sheets were obtainable only from France, whence they had to be imported at vast expense and no doubt enormous practical difficulty. An inventory of the Osterley contents drawn up in 1782 shows that the first large plate of English-made mirror glass in the house is the one over the chimneypiece of the State Bedroom which was decorated and furnished at a later date than the Drawing Room.

56 *Designs by Adam for furniture and fittings intended for Lord Derby's London house, from* The Works in Architecture, *vol. II, 1789*

In mirror design Adam achieved one of his most original forms. Instead of restricting himself to the oval or rectangular frames which are typical of his earlier career, we find him in his period of mastery using the glass itself as a kind of foundation on which he assembles a delicate, cobwebby tracery of decoration carried out in gilded wood, plaster or metal composition. A fine example can be seen in the Music Room at Kenwood, Hampstead (although this design is not known to be by Adam himself).

The provision of a room specifically set aside for home music-making became an increasingly noticeable feature of house-planning after 1750. Before then, music had been performed in hall, long gallery or private parlour. But private concert-giving was on the increase, and a distinctive apartment in which to hold such entertainments became an essential feature of many large houses. 'After thus mentioning the uses of ancient apartments, it is necessary to enumerate those additions which modern life requires . . . 4th. The Music-room.' (Humphry Repton, *Observations on the Theory and Practice of Landscape Gardening including some remarks on . . . Architecture*, 1803.) The purpose of a music room is often indicated by the decoration – carved, painted or plaster trophies of musical instruments on walls or ceiling (especially the classical lyre and the syrinx or pan-pipes), or carved or painted groups showing Orpheus and the Muses or the musical contest between Apollo and the unfortunate Marsyas (who lost the competition and paid for his presumption by being flayed alive). Adam himself created several notable music rooms, of which the one at Number 20, Portman Square, London (now the Courtauld Institute of Art) may well be considered the finest of all his interiors.

However, for the country house visitor there may be two other important clues to the original function of the music room. First, in deference to its original function, it may still contain an early keyboard instrument such as a harpsichord. This instrument, with its distinctive twanging sounds produced by a plucking action, is several centuries old, and may also be found in two other forms known as the virginals (popular during the sixteenth and early seventeenth centuries, basically oblong, and placed on a table for playing) and the spinet, triangular or 'leg-of-mutton' in shape and at its peak of popularity from about 1680 to 1720. When Pepys remarks: 'This day my tryangle, which was put in tune yesterday, did please me greatly', he is referring to his triangular-shaped spinet. The cases of English-made eighteenth-century harpsichords and spinets are generally veneered in plain walnut or mahogany, in contrast to Continental ones which tend to be much more highly decorated.

The second and more obvious clue to a music room may be the presence of an organ. The popularity of Handel's music and of his organ concertos in particular (he was already revered long before his death in 1759) led to a fashionable craze – one can hardly call it anything else – for small but beautifully-cased organs designed for houses rather than for churches. For these instruments, which are called chamber organs, several notable architects and others designed cases; they included Kent, Thomas Johnson, Chippendale (who published several chamber organ designs in the 1762 edition of the *Director*), and Adam himself. Sometimes the organ case was incorporated within the decoration of the room; this was successfully done, for example, by Adam's rival James Wyatt at Heaton Hall, by the simple but effective device of continuing the cornice of the room round the top of the projecting organ case without a break.

Certain other features of interior planning and decoration which are characteristic of Adam remain to be noticed. For important apartments he frequently introduces an apse at either one or both ends of the room, and almost as often emphasises this feature by means of an ornamental beam supported on columns, forming a kind of screen to the apse. This too derives from classical precedents; its use in England goes back to Inigo Jones, and the Palladians also employed it on occasion, but Adam was the first to introduce it so consistently into his interiors. His spatial mastery is unquestioned, and is perhaps seen to best advantage at Syon. In the richly-decorated Ante-Room with its floor of coloured scagliola and its columns said to have been dredged from the bottom of the Tiber at Rome (one or two may have been, but the remainder are almost certainly imitation), Adam entirely succeeds in giving the impression that the room is square. Actually it is an awkward 36 by 30 feet, but he has achieved the illusion by setting four of the columns 8 feet away from the wall and making them carry a beam topped with classical figures. Similarly, in the original Tudor Long Gallery he has used an intricate ceiling pattern of linked squares and octagons to deceive the eye and lead us into thinking that this impossibly long room is broader and shorter than it really is. To further the deception he has also broken up the interminable wall into repeated units which echo the device of the Roman triumphal arch. The Syon Long Gallery is probably the room in which Adam's grotesque style can be studied to best advantage.

The sheer variety of Adam's ceiling designs is astounding, and in them his developing style can again be traced. At Kenwood, in the magnificent Library, he even developed a type of ceiling never previously seen on such a large scale in an English interior before – an enormous barrel vault, which he frankly calls 'extremely beautiful, and much more perfect than that which is commonly called the cove ceiling'. (But the barrel vault was not unknown; there is an impressive one, for example, in the Long Gallery at Chasleton, Oxfordshire, a house built in 1603.)

The outlines of Adam's ceiling decorations are frequently mirrored (in essence though not necessarily in detail) in the design of the carpet beneath, or by other means; for example, in the Entrance Hall at Osterley the ceiling pattern is echoed in the patterns of the marble flooring. Contemporary prints and paintings show that many eighteenth-century rooms remained uncarpeted, exposing the plain wooden floorboards. It is noteworthy that Adam's carpets do not reach to the edge of the room but leave a space all round the walls,

57 *The magnificent Ante-room at Syon, described by Adam as being intended 'for the attendance of the servants . . . and also for that of tradesmen &c.'*

where (as we have already noted) the furniture would be ranged. Obviously to him the idea of pieces of furniture standing on his carpets and interrupting their design was totally repugnant.

That carpets and ceilings should have matching patterns was just one facet of Adam's firm belief that every room should be designed as an entity, and that the different features of its decoration should harmonise with each other. For this reason he paid as close attention to the careful design of such items as chimney-pieces, grates, door handles and keyhole escutcheons (surrounds) as he did to the general design of the rooms themselves. Even the decoration of certain pieces of furniture reflects the rooms in which they are placed; for example, the lyre-back design of the Osterley Eating Room chairs is emphasised on a larger scale in the panels of grotesques beneath which they are intended to stand.

During Adam's lifetime thousands of painstaking and exquisitely hand-coloured drawings of details such as these, as well as of his larger architectural undertakings, were produced by himself, his brother James and their office staff. After the death of the last surviving brother William in 1821 some 9,000 of these drawings eventually became the property of Sir John Soane and are still preserved in bound volumes at Soane's London house, now a museum (see p. 152).

A number of the designs were published in book form during Adam's own lifetime in two huge volumes entitled *The Works in Architecture of Robert and James Adam*. They appeared in 1773 and 1779, a third volume being published posthumously in 1822. This important work was really the brothers' manifesto, just as *Vitruvius Britannicus* had been that of Colen Campbell and the Palladians. Their main beliefs are set out in an illuminating preface to Volume One, and it is from *The Works in Architecture* that the various comments by Robert Adam himself which appear in this chapter are taken.

The Works in Architecture contains engravings of some of Adam's finest furniture, including pieces at Osterley and Syon. In contrast the final phase of his furniture style, which dates from about 1778 to his death in 1792, shows a falling off in both quantity and quality. As regards the latter, everything becomes more refined, simplified and standardised, while for decoration he seems to have relied increasingly on either painted or metal ornament. As regards the decline in quantity, two main reasons appear. The first was a fall in demand; due partly to the American Revolution and the war resulting from it, patrons could no longer afford to commission expensive furniture from Adam. The second reason was, quite simply, competition.

It is perhaps not generally appreciated that by the 1770s Adam's style in furniture had been fully assimilated by the great cabinet-makers of the day, including Thomas Chippendale, who were well able to copy it on their own and to produce pieces in 'Adam style' without necessarily any reference to Adam himself. Most people are aware of Adam's aim to unify his work by ensuring that even the smallest details of interior decoration should relate to the wider architectural and decorative unity of the whole. But his opportunities for applying these principles to the furniture as well were in fact very limited, and the number of houses for which he was invited to supply a complete range of furniture designs was remarkably small, not more than five at the most. Far more often the patron would give the contract for designing and supplying the furniture to a cabinet-maker such as Chippendale or John Linnell.

The extent to which Chippendale successfully appropriated part of Adam's mantle for himself presents us with yet another aspect of his versatile genius. A number of pieces of furniture exist which for many years were supposed to have been made by Chippendale to the designs of Adam. This was especially true of furniture at Harewood House, and conveniently overlooked the fact that while no designs or bills for furniture there by Adam are known to exist, there *are* bills amounting to about £3,000-worth of furniture supplied by Chippendale, plus evidence that the original total was nearer £6,000. We now accept the fact that this Harewood furniture, together with other pieces in other houses, was in fact designed and made in Chippendale's workshop and that Adam

58 *Commode of about 1770, in the style of Adam but attributed to Chippendale*

had no hand in it, though it is undeniably in his style. At the same time there is evidence that in other instances he and Chippendale did in fact collaborate, and that on those occasions Adam supplied designs which Chippendale then executed.

Furniture of the later Adam period is marked by a return to popularity of marquetry, which had fallen somewhat out of favour in the middle years of the eighteenth century, and by the introduction of new woods of which the best known and most characteristic is the warm honey-coloured satinwood, coming from both the West and East Indies. Mahogany was still popular but now came from a new source, Honduras, and was lighter in colour and weight, as well as being of slightly inferior quality.

Most thorough-going Adam-type furniture was designed with specific patrons in mind, and such patrons were, of course, rich. Someone was needed who could adapt it to the requirements of the not-so-rich who nevertheless wanted to keep up as far as possible with current trends in fashion. This adaptation came about through the work of George Hepplewhite and Thomas Sheraton.

As in the case of Chippendale, there are many popular misconceptions about these two craftsmen. Firstly, their style is not at all the same thing as 'Regency', as we shall see. Secondly, they had no personal contact; indeed Hepplewhite was dead probably before Sheraton ever came to work in London. Thirdly, and most importantly, no single piece of furniture has ever been positively identified as having been made by Hepplewhite himself, much less by Sheraton who, although originally trained as a cabinet-maker in the north of England, apparently never practised his trade at all once he had settled in London. The real significance of both men rests in the books of designs that, following the now established tradition, were eventually published under their names.

First to appear was Hepplewhite's *The Cabinet Maker and Upholsterer's Guide*, in fact produced posthumously by his widow in 1788 (he died in 1786). We know little about him except that he came to London from apprenticeship to the worthy firm of Gillows of Lancaster, and that by 1760 he had his own establishment in Cripplegate. Probably he was not very successful in life, or he would have moved to an area more fashionable for cabinet-makers such as St Martin's Lane. However, there was no denying the success of his book, which had a second edition in 1789 and a third in 1794. It was popular because it fully met the demand for elegant yet serviceable furniture in a toned-down version of Adam's manner from which Hepplewhite was careful to omit the heavier classical elements. Moreover it was the most useful and comprehensive work of its kind since the publication of the *Director* 34 years previously, and like that earlier publication was the means of spreading the new style throughout the country.

Hepplewhite is perhaps most celebrated for his popularisation of the shield-back chair. He certainly did not invent this form – the original shape may well

Corner Bason Stands.

59 *Designs for washstands, from Sheraton's* Cabinet-Maker and Upholsterer's Guide, *3 ed., 1802. Water would not be piped to the left-hand example, but stored ready for use in the small cistern*

have been introduced by Adam – but he did bring it to a high pitch of elegant excellence. The back itself is raised on two short uprights above the seat level and the central splat takes a variety of forms in which the influence of Adam-style ornament prevails. Hepplewhite, however, seems to have been responsible for introducing one new decorative motif which became very popular for a time, not only on chairs but on other pieces of furniture and even ladies' head-dresses; this was the Prince of Wales's feathers (three ostrich plumes arranged in the form of a crown). Apart from this innovation and the shield-back itself Hepplewhite's chairs are still very much in the Adam manner with square or cylindrical legs ending in spade or peg feet, the arms, seat-rail and back often being carved with small motifs such as husks, paterae and crossed palm leaves; fluting and reeding are also usual, the latter apparently being the more popular of the two. The shield-backs themselves could also be stuffed and upholstered, though in Hepplewhite's book chairs of this type are for some curious reason called 'cabriole'.

Hepplewhite's book also promoted two other forms of chair-back, the oval and the very beautiful but less common heart-shape. The chairs in his designs do not have stretchers, though it is obvious from existing examples that, just as in the case of Chippendale, provincial makers put them in, in order to give greater strength and stability. There is a good deal of fashionable French influence discernible in some of the designs, notably those for elegant window-seats and a curious type of settee called a 'confidante', but also many practical ideas for pieces which are basically more functional and useful than decorative.

For example, Hepplewhite was the first designer of stature to deal convincingly with unromantic but necessary items such as washstands, Chippendale having only nodded briefly in their direction (see p. 94) and Adam having apparently loftily ignored all bedroom furniture except for the Osterley state bed and two others. The Hepplewhite chest-of-drawers, with its splayed bracket feet and bowed or serpentine front, was the final metamorphosis of the elegant Chippendale 'dressing commode', reduced to essentials and to a form that still survives today both in originals and in imitations. Adam's ostentatious dining-room group of side-table and urns is reduced in Hepplewhite's *Guide* to a single sideboard with capacious drawers, setting the pattern for very many similar bow- or serpentine-fronted pieces; these have four or six legs, though some experts assert that the four-legged variety are in fact dressing-tables intended for bedroom use. And it is in the *Guide* that we meet with the first illustration of that most useful and highly popular small table known as a 'Pembroke', normally oval or rectangular, with a falling flap along each of its long sides and very often a small drawer. We are indebted to Sheraton for the information (right or wrong, who can tell) that the name is that of a Mrs Pembroke who first ordered such a table to be made. If this is so, the lady must join the company of that gallant Captain and respected Archbishop who are also said to have lent their names to the Davenport and the Canterbury respectively.

Thomas Sheraton was born in 1751 at Stockton-on-Tees and apparently achieved the status of journeyman cabinet-maker before coming to settle in London about 1790; however, he does not seem to have practised his trade after leaving the North, but instead to have eked out a precarious living as a drawing-master and a supplier of designs to other cabinet-makers. The undoubted success of his best-known work, *The Cabinet Maker and Upholsterer's Drawing Book* (a title confusingly similar to that of Hepplewhite's *Guide*), which appeared in four parts between 1791 and 1794, was unfortunately not enough to stave off insanity and an early death in 1806.

Sheraton promoted the square-backed chair with straight, horizontal top (the outline sometimes softened by slightly sloping 'shoulders'), angularity and straight lines being emphasised by parallel uprights spaced evenly within the frame of the back and giving a window-like effect. That this was popular is

60 *Hepplewhite-style shield-back chair with Prince of Wales feathers motif and
unfashionable stretchers. (V. and A. Museum)*

borne out by the fact that the third (1794) edition of Hepplewhite's *Guide* included designs for square-backs for the first time, presumably as a sop to current taste; indeed Sheraton himself had already remarked rather patronisingly (in the preface to his *Drawing Book*) that the Hepplewhite chair designs were not in 'the newest taste'. Apart from general outline, however, Sheraton's own chair designs are again much in the Adam/Hepplewhite manner, though perhaps more elegant. It is in fact this aura of elegance, largely French-inspired, that in the absence of more concrete evidence seems to mark out a Sheraton-type piece from one conceived under the slightly earlier influence of Hepplewhite.

For it is indeed often very difficult, if not impossible, to assign a particular piece of late eighteenth-century furniture to the direct influence of either Hepplewhite or Sheraton, apart from chairs. Certainly there are one or two 'trade marks' associated especially with Sheraton. Not much of the fussy curtaining and looped drapery which he loved to append to a wide variety of pieces has survived, if indeed it ever existed to any extent outside his designs. But he promoted the French idea of painted furniture (the ornament being painted onto the surface rather than being applied or executed in marquetry) and he also had a marked liking for pieces containing mechanisms of varying complexity. Simplest of these was the tambour panel (thin slats of wood stuck to a canvas backing), a device whose application to desk, dressing table, side-board and so on enabled such pieces to be made in a rounded or 'cylinder' form where previously the use of flat doors and lids would have dictated an angular shape. The progress of Sheraton's insanity is marked among other things by the increasingly frenzied Heath Robinson character of his mechanical designs and by the fussiness of his general approach, giving an unmistakable impression of a powerful but sadly disordered mind. This, however, is a later manifestation and is not noticeable in the *Drawing Book*.

But there is of course a very large class of late eighteenth- and early nineteenth-century furniture which cannot be assigned to the direct influence of either Hepplewhite or Sheraton but is instead derived from a subtle mixture of both. That two so very popular works as their books should have had a strong combined influence throughout the country was only to be expected. Therefore, unless one feels particularly confident, it is usually as well to avoid pinning one or the other label to furniture of the period, remembering also that other designers were on the scene as well. *The Cabinet-Maker's London Book of Prices* was published in 1788 by a craftsman named Thomas Shearer and contains a number of designs for useful and functional pieces which were evidently popular, such as the 'lady's screen desk', a small secretaire on an open stand at which a lady could sit by the fireside and write, warming her feet whilst her face was screened from the flames. One would have expected such an idea to be pure Sheraton. Both Shearer and Sheraton, like Hepplewhite, pay attention to the mundane demands of the daily toilet and produce similarly serviceable

61 *Sheraton-style chair with painted decoration and cane seat. (V. and A. Museum)*

62   *Satinwood secretaire with painted decoration, and small stand, both in Hepplewhite/Sheraton style*

designs for washstands and dressing tables. It is in this area of purely functional furniture that it becomes especially difficult, if not impossible, to differentiate between the styles.

Both Hepplewhite and Sheraton obviously wished to share their style with the world at large and hoped that others would follow their lead. Adam, one feels, would have preferred to keep his style to himself. But this was obviously impossible, and indeed it was comparatively easy for others, often of far lesser ability, to copy the Adam style. In the 1773 preface to the first volume of *The Works in Architecture* the brothers show their awareness of the fact that they already had imitators. Their most serious rival was James Wyatt who jumped onto the Adam bandwaggon at the outset of his career, though he later became more interested in Gothic. But Wyatt was an architect of ability who, although undeniably helping himself to many of the familiar Adam ingredients, nevertheless managed to reconstitute them into a recognisable mixture of his own. In later years he defended himself against the charge of plagiarism by asserting, rather lamely: 'When I came back from Italy I found the public taste corrupted by the Adams, and I was obliged to comply with it.' The best examples of Wyatt echoing Adam (but not merely imitating him) are Heaton Hall and Heveningham Hall. Here can be seen to advantage what is perhaps the most characteristic feature of Wyatt's personal Neo-classical style – his ability to understate, to leave entirely blank quite large areas of wall space which Adam would have felt compelled to fill in with grotesques and/or other ornament. Wyatt understood the value of such areas in complementing or highlighting the ornament, which, it should be noted, he also tends to use more sparingly than Adam.

Even Adam could not remain untouched by the general enthusiasm for Gothic. His chief essay in it is Culzean Castle (Ayrshire), begun in 1777 and completed in 1790. Culzean is impressively romantic in appearance, an original old castle having been successfully enlarged in a manner that shows Robert Adam well able to compete with more Gothic-minded architects of the period (though his drawings show that in fact Gothic had originally been one of his youthful enthusiasms). The interior, however, is pure classical Adam, its chief feature being a wonderful oval staircase with a cast-iron balustrade incorporating a typical yet uniquely elegant urn motif (also to be found, for example, on the garden staircase at Osterley).

Though this book is primarily about country houses we cannot leave the Adam brothers without a brief reference to the part they played in town planning and urban building. In this they were speculators and put a great deal of money into building, on the banks of the Thames next to Somerset House (the work of Adam's critic Sir William Chambers, though not in fact built until later), a terrace of gracious houses with great arched warehouses beneath them at river level, and a complex of streets behind. This estate was called the Adelphi (Greek for brothers) and it survived until the 1930s, when to our national

63   *Heveningham Hall, Suffolk. By Sir Robert Taylor, 1779, with interiors by James Wyatt, 1781–1784. The Entrance Hall – Adam's style superbly understated by Wyatt*

shame a later generation of speculators was allowed to demolish most of it in the name of commercial progress. The houses on the terrace fronting the river were treated on the exterior as a single architectural composition with one long façade common to all. One house still remaining today in nearby Adam Street shows how Adam applied features of his interior decoration to the exteriors as well, for the familiar honeysuckle motif appears in a series of large vertical reliefs down the front of the building. The nucleus of the complex behind the riverside terrace was a building specially designed as the head-quarters of the then newly-formed Royal Society of Arts, and happily this too survives. The Adam brothers also built similar schemes of London town houses in Portland Place and Fitzroy Square, parts of which still remain. The drawing room from the Adelphi house of David Garrick, the famous actor, has been preserved and rebuilt in the Victoria and Albert Museum; it has a fine ceiling which has recently been restored in its original colours.

Towards the latter part of his life Robert Adam lost some of his popularity in England and commissions there declined, partly due to the general drain on finances caused by the American War of Independence. To compensate for this he became much more deeply involved with work in his native Scotland, including the replanning of a large part of the city of Edinburgh. He died suddenly in London in 1792 and was buried in Westminster Abbey.

At the conclusion of this chapter let Robert and James Adam speak again for themselves in this final extract from the preface to *The Works in Architecture*:

If we have any claim to approbation, we found it on this alone: That we flatter ourselves we have been able to seize with some degree of success the beautiful spirit of antiquity, and to transfuse it with novelty and variety through all our numerous works.

64 *Belvoir Castle, Leicestershire. By James Wyatt, 1816. This view across the staircase-well shows us Regency Gothic at its finest, including the cast-iron balustrade*

CHAPTER SIX

Regency Restraint

*I*N STRICT historical terms the Regency of George, Prince of Wales, began in 1811 and lasted until 1820 when he ascended the throne as George IV. In terms of art history, however, the period is a good deal more elastic and imprecise, beginning in the late 1780s and continuing through the reigns of George IV (1820–30) and his brother William IV (1830–37), up to the accession of the young Victoria in 1837. Such a lengthy time-span must inevitably cover certain stylistic changes, despite the blanket title of 'Regency', and there are now good grounds for belief that we ought in particular to be giving much more attention to the short reign of William IV as an important period for the fine and applied arts in its own right. However, blanket titles are useful, and there is no doubt that the later years of the eighteenth century and the first four decades of the nineteenth do share certain stylistic trends which it is still convenient to classify generally as Regency.

Inevitably certain artists also lived through the transition from eighteenth to nineteenth century. Among the most notable of these was James Wyatt, whom we have already met in a double capacity, the first as an architect in a personalised version of the Adam style. Always sensitive to public taste, Wyatt recognised by the 1790s that the vogue for this type of building and decoration were both played out. His last house in the classical manner was begun in 1798; this is Dodington (Gloucestershire), a house characterised both inside and out by a noble simplicity, completed by the owner according to Wyatt's plans and designs after the latter's unnecessary death in a carriage accident (1813).

In his second role, that of purveyor of the Gothic, Wyatt continued to work enthusiastically and at the time of his death was engaged in completing the remodelling of Belvoir Castle, the Duke of Rutland's Leicestershire seat. Work here had begun in 1801 and resulted in a deceptively medieval-looking pile, less of a tour-de-force than Fonthill perhaps, but more successful because more durably built. Although much of the interior was gutted by fire in 1816, it was immediately rebuilt in the spirit if not the letter of Wyatt's own work; his own brand of Gothic – more delicate and scholarly than that of Horace Walpole, though no less enjoyable – is especially noticeable in the Entrance Passage and adjoining hall, inevitably and romantically named the Guardroom. On the other hand the decorations in the Saloon, designed and carried out after the fire by Wyatt's son Matthew, are in the French style of Louis XIV and actually incorporate gilded panelling taken from a château formerly belonging to Louis' mistress Madame de Maintenon. This 'Louis Quatorze' style set something of a fashion, for it continued to be used into the early Victorian period, though soon becoming indistinguishable from the florid French Rococo style more properly associated with the period of Louis XV and Madame Pompadour.

Ashridge, Hertfordshire, was another of Wyatt's huge Gothic mansions (begun 1806), much more akin to Fonthill than Belvoir and – since it still stands – giving us valuable insight into the dramatic impact that Fonthill must have made on all who saw it. Ashridge incorporates a spacious chapel whose lofty fan-vaulted roof is probably Wyatt's finest existing essay in medievalism. Even larger than Ashridge was the recently-demolished Eaton Hall in Cheshire, a gigantic house begun in 1803 for Earl Grosvenor by William Porden. Bristling with spires, pinnacles and crockets, the house looked like a huge wedding cake; its unscholarly excesses were too much for the more serious-

65 *Ashridge, Hertfordshire. By James Wyatt, 1808. Castellated Regency grandeur*

minded Victorians, and later in the nineteenth century the architect Alfred Waterhouse was asked to tone the whole thing down.

However, it would be a mistake to suppose that the Regency Gothic style was confined to large mansions. Many smaller country houses may be found in which miniature towers, pointed-arch windows, imitation arrow-slits and apologies for battlements proclaim the influence of Gothic, powerfully aided at the time by the novels of Sir Walter Scott, the first, *Waverley*, appearing in 1814. (Scott is often thought of as a Victorian, yet he died in 1832, five years before the Victorian era began.) Indeed, modern research shows that the architecture and furnishings of Scott's own house Abbotsford (begun 1822), which was built in a conscious revival of 'Scottish Baronial' style, must be counted as being extremely influential to the Gothic movement. However, much of the interior of Abbotsford is over-heavy with the dark panelling and carved wooden ornament that is more typical of Victorian Gothic, whilst on the whole the Regency preference was for a lighter style looking backwards to Strawberry Hill rather than forwards. In this style, pointed archways and imitation fan-vaulting in wood or plaster helped to emphasise the cheerfully unconvincing illusion of medievalism.

The miniature Gothic castle-house was a type of dwelling which had a special fascination for the great John Nash (1752–1835), and indeed he was celebrated for his work in this style long before he became the favourite architect of the Prince Regent. Though his own house, East Cowes Castle on the Isle of Wight, has now disappeared, others which he built remain. One such is Luscombe (Devonshire), whose pseudo-medieval exterior belies the classical décor inside, showing that at this period a combination of conflicting styles was still generally acceptable.

This conflict, however, is not visible from outside. For Luscombe, East Cowes and other houses of their type were not merely imitation Gothic castles. They were specifically designed to fit into the landscape in a picturesque manner, and indeed the deliberate cult of the picturesque in architecture was something that began in the 1790s. Men like Nash and Humphry Repton (the landscape gardener and, for a time, Nash's partner) believed that it was important to design and build houses in close relationship to the surrounding landscape, so that they should form an harmonious composition with it, as though in a painting. By no means all the houses designed with this theory in mind were in the castle style. Nash himself built several of a vaguely Italian villa type, with round, conically-roofed towers and very deep eaves; one still surviving is Cronkhill near Shrewsbury.

But far more important to the picturesque ideal was the rediscovery of the cottage, not only as a suitably interesting feature of a picturesque landscape but also, as Sir John Summerson has remarked, 'as an architectural toy with an intrinsic interest of its own'.* John Nash's chief contribution to cottage archi-

* *Architecture in Britain, 1530 to 1830*, p. 294.

66   *Cronkhill, Shropshire. By John Nash, 1802. A small Italian-style house in a picturesque setting*

tecture was a complete village, Blaise Hamlet near Bristol, now a National Trust property. Here the houses are arranged round a village green, their front doors purposely facing away from each other so as to discourage gossip. However, these were cottages for working people, as opposed to pretty retreats for people of more substantial means attracted by the fashionable cry of 'back to Nature' – but not too far back. The popularity of the cottage ideal is stressed by the number of books of designs for cottages that appeared between 1790 and 1810. Many could equally well serve as gatekeepers' lodges, gamekeepers' cottages and so on, for these were designed on exactly the same principles, as also were dairies, dovecotes, outhouses and the like.

On the other hand the dividing line between such cottage dwellings on the one hand and the smaller genteel country villas on the other was very thin. Though often pretentious, they all had the merit of great diversity. Almost no two are exactly alike – indeed, architects did their best to avoid this – yet, despite wide differences in size and appearance, through them all runs the unifying thread of the picturesque. The term 'cottage orné' is often used to identify them.

One of the best places to study and enjoy not only this sense of unity in diversity but also the development of the cottage/villa idea into that of the smaller house proper is at Tunbridge Wells in Kent. Here in 1828 Decimus Burton accepted a commission to lay out and build an entire residential area called the Calverley Estate, a fascinating slice of parkland bordered on one side only by a series of individually-designed smallish houses. Here too we may see fine examples of those typical Regency features, the verandah and the cast-iron ornamental balcony. The first is a Regency peculiarity that came into fashion quite suddenly and probably originated with the contemporary interest in India; inspiration for the second, on the other hand, seems to have come from Italy. In a sense we may perhaps look on the Calverley Estate as an early manifestation of the garden suburb, though this is a concept which properly belongs to the twentieth century.

With diversity in appearance there came also diversity in planning. The smaller Regency country house, whether in the Gothic, picturesque or classical styles, is to our way of thinking considerably and agreeably more compact and convenient than anything that had gone before it. In printed plans of the period, dining and drawing rooms are marked as such, and very often open out at each side of the entrance hall. New designations, not encountered earlier, are shown – parlour, morning room, study and (in larger houses) billiards room.* (The smoking room did not appear until the Victorian era was fairly launched.) The kitchen was at the back of the house and was often comple- mented by washhouse/bakehouse/scullery. The upper floor or floors, to which the servants had access by their own stairs, were given over to the bedrooms of family and staff. There were no bathrooms as we understand the term and washing was performed in the bedrooms, water being carried up for the purpose. However, one or two plans of the period do show small ground- floor rooms mysteriously marked 'bath' – presumably these were of the cold plunge variety, then as later considered by some to be invigorating and health- giving. (At Brighton the Prince Regent had a bath like a small swimming pool into which sea water was pumped direct.)

The appealing modernity of this type of house was often completed by the provision of a conservatory attached to the house. This fashion arose from a happy combination of (1) late eighteenth-century realisation by gardeners that plants need sunshine and light as well as heat; (2) the discovery that glass and cast iron, aided by lead, could be used together to make interesting new

*But some billiards rooms were extant by the 1770s, while the game itself was being played in the seventeenth century.

structures; (3) the Regency fashion for growing plants indoors, as a result of which the jardinière or plant container was introduced for the first time.

The furnishings of any house, whatever its period, are normally a mixture of old and new, and to this the smaller Regency country house or villa was no exception. For instance, in the drawing room the useful and well-established Pembroke table was now supplemented by the sofa table, distinguished from the Pembroke by its rectangular shape, its generally larger size and by having its flaps along the short sides. It often had two drawers and stood either on end supports connected by a horizontal stretcher or on a central pedestal from which sprouted four curving feet. Such pieces now moved freely on brass castors, for which the most popular Regency housing was a simulated lion's paw; brass rings, plain or hanging from lions' jaws, were the most popular form of drawer-handle.

The sofa table rapidly became one of the most useful pieces of furniture in the house, and in poor though genteel families frequently did duty as a dining table. Yet, as its name implies, it had developed in conjunction with the sofa proper, at a convenient height to be used by a reclining lady. For a looser,

67 *Rosewood sofa table inlaid with brass, about 1820*

simpler fashion in dress (plain high-waisted muslin gowns), due partly to the French Revolution and partly to a revival of the Greek classical ideal, meant that ladies could now spend more time in the drawing room reclining gracefully rather than sitting. Just how gracefully can be seen in Jacques David's famous portrait of Madame Récamier. The Regency sofa was perfectly adapted to this form of relaxation, having a scrolled end-piece against which the lady could lean, a low back along which she could lay a languidly elegant arm, and the inevitable round bolster on which she could support her elbow whilst reading Miss Austen's latest novel. The sofa was low and usually stood on legs whose sharp concave curve repeated that found in the legs of other pieces of the time such as the sofa table itself and a variety of chairs.

This curve is especially interesting, for it calls to mind the shape of a cavalry-man's sabre and is a reminder of the strong military influence to be found in much furniture and decoration of the time; this was of course a direct result of the Napoleonic wars which began in 1793 and lasted with interruptions until Waterloo in 1815. We shall note a number of other instances in which this influence appears, for it was inevitable that a social upheaval of such magnitude should have widespread and far-reaching effects on almost every aspect of European life. (However, although this type of curved leg did actually come to be called a 'sabre leg', even sometimes 'scimitar leg', its true origins lay in Greek classical furniture; see p. 149.)

On the typical Regency chair the sabre shape may be confined to either front or back legs, or found in all four. The arms are set relatively high and have scrolled ends, the back is square and low, the tops of the back uprights also being scrolled over. The back itself very frequently consists of a panel at the top, below which is a space occupied only by a connecting bar. Cane seats, covered by squab cushions, made a comeback for the first time since the seventeenth century, and cane was also sometimes used for the infilling of back and arms. Rosewood (from Brazil and India) now began to rival mahogany in popularity and decoration was often carved, though more opulent chairs tended to be painted and gilded. Fluting and reeding continued to be used, as did some of the old classical motifs such as the anthemion, but these were less delicate than in the Adam and Hepplewhite eras and became increasingly chunky as the Victorian era approached.

On some Regency chairs a carved moulding resembling rope has given them the name of 'Trafalgar' chairs, for obvious reasons. Yet even before Nelson's famous victory of 1805 his other naval successes and personal popularity were being reflected in furniture details – not only the rope motif but such things as anchors, dolphins, and even that old favourite the lion mask. More immediately associated with the battle of Trafalgar are the signs of public mourning for Nelson's death – the 'ebonising' (painting black) of chairs, the carving of back splats to represent his coffin draperies, the inlaying into mahogany chair frames of thin lines of ebony.

In the dining room the side-table with flanking pedestals was still to be found and indeed seems to have enjoyed a slight revival in popularity in about 1805–1810. But the convenience of the compact type developed by Hepplewhite and Sheraton was too obvious to be ignored, though the simple bow-fronted, four- or six-legged variety gradually became a much more ponderous object resting on solid end-pieces often with an equally solid and heavy back-piece instead of the light brass rail typical of Hepplewhite. Knife-boxes, standing now on the sideboard itself, were sometimes retained, but some had lost their graceful urn-like shape and became square boxes tapering towards the foot. The brass rail at the back of the sideboard supported plates, if and when it was retained.

In the not-so-rich Regency household a useful yet fashionable substitute for the sideboard was the chiffonier, originally a type of French clothes cupboard but by about 1805 having become a cupboard pedestal with double doors surmounted by a back frame fitted with a shelf. The top of the pedestal might be fitted with a marble slab, a mirror fitted into the back frame, the top shelf completed by a brass rail, and the cupboard doors, instead of being solid, filled in with the typical brass 'chicken wire' backed by pleated green silk that is also

68 *Sideboard, about 1810. The new compact type developed by Hepplewhite and Shearer*

to be found on bookcases and similar pieces of the period.

Sideboard, chiffonier, chairs and other Regency furniture are often decorated with thin inlaid strips of brass. This fashion, beginning about 1815, was of French origin, and there was also a revival of interest in the French technique of overall brass decoration known as boulle. This technique, first developed at the court of Louis XIV by André Charles Boulle (from which it gets its name – there is no justification for using the Victorian Germanic spelling 'buhl') is really a form of marquetry in which thin sheet brass and tortoiseshell are used instead of wood, and with it goes much use of heavy ormolu mounts. Of all the French furniture fashions introduced into this country after 1660, boulle was the one which made the least impact at the time, and it failed to attain any kind of popularity until the 1820s, when George IV's enthusiasm for French seventeenth-century art communicated itself to fashionable society. Some Regency chairs also have brass motifs, such as the anthemion, incorporated into their backs.

> The common useful dining tables are upon pillar and claws, generally four claws to each pillar, with brass castors. A dining table of this kind may be made to any size, by having a sufficient quantity of pillar and claw parts, for between each of them is a loose flap . . . easily taken off and put aside.

Thus wrote Sheraton in 1803. But round dining tables on similar supports were now also in use, the central pillar usually being a fairly massive affair. Round tables of the same type were also used in libraries, having alternating real and dummy drawers around their tops (wedge-shaped drawers, though less usual, are also found); these are sometimes known as drum tables.

Common to drawing room, dining room or library was that most familiar of all Regency pieces, the round convex mirror in gilt plaster frame, decorated with small gilt balls and surmounted by a carved plaster or wooden eagle. Such a mirror is sometimes completed by candle branches and a decorative pendant of acanthus leaves. Again it is difficult to avoid the conclusion that this eagle originally reflected the preoccupation with Napoleonic glory and French militarism (it seems actually to have been introduced from France round about 1800), though no doubt it later became a mere decorative convention. Another Napoleonic motif which occasionally appears on Regency furniture is the fasces, the axe in a bundle of rods that was the symbol of office of the Roman consuls and was readopted by Napoleon in his earlier capacity as First Consul. (It was later to reappear for a time in Italy under Mussolini.)

A more direct influence from military life was to be found in the Regency bedroom. The tent or field bed, in its simplest form, had a post rising from the middle of one side of the bed-frame; from the top of this post hung draperies which were arranged over the head- and foot-boards in a tent-like manner. In more elaborate versions curved iron rods rising from the four posts supported the hangings to make a proper tester. In still more elaborate beds the iron

69   *Rosewood bookcase with ormolu mounts and brass wire grilles, about 1810*

rods supported a central dome. The specifically 'French' or 'sofa' bedstead stood against the wall, and with heavily scrolled ends did indeed look more like a sofa than a bed; the draperies were arranged on the same principle as in the simple tent bed, though sometimes they hung from an ornamental half-dome canopy fixed to the wall.

Bedroom furniture as a whole changed little from the simpler lines laid down by Hepplewhite. One of the most interesting printed designs of the period is for a bedroom in which the bed itself is set into an alcove, the sides of which are formed by two recesses fitted with drawers and clothes pegs – surely one of the earliest instances of built-in furniture in the modern sense. A popular item of bedroom furniture was now the swing-mirror set in a frame, or cheval glass (cheval = horse = a frame, hence clothes-horse).

The observer of Regency furniture will very soon notice the large number of pieces that are decorated with Egyptian heads and even mock hieroglyphics. The heads are usually surmounting tapering pilasters, and if the same observer looks more closely at the bottom of those pilasters he will almost certainly see something very odd – the feet belonging to the heads, separated from them by an impossible distance and presumably by an equally impossibly elongated and strait-jacketed body. This (though in fact based on ancient classical precedent), is probably the most ridiculous and unintentionally hilarious convention in the whole history of furniture and its decoration, a subject not normally noted for humour.

All comedy apart, the Egyptian influence is one of the more important ingredients of Regency furniture style. Interest in Egyptian art was not entirely new, but the added impetus given to it during the Regency period was once again largely due to Napoleon and specifically to his Egyptian campaign. Official archaeologists were attached to the French army in Egypt; they were headed by a Baron Denon, who in 1804 published the results of his discoveries which were read throughout Europe. In England the Egyptian vogue was at its height during the period 1804–10, and resulted in some strange architectural and decorative curiosities. 'Egyptian' interiors were created, with columns having palm-leaf capitals instead of the usual classical ones, and there were even wallpaper designs composed of objects such as sphinxes and mummy cases.

The curious upward tapering associated with the Egyptian temple style is sometimes reflected in bulky items of furniture such as bookcases, and there are many different uses for two- or three-dimensional Egyptian figures in wood or painted plaster, as distinct from the head-and-feet-in-tube variety. Fairly popular also was a form of small round table standing on a central pillar designed to look like a palm tree and flanked by winged cats. (Another interesting Egyptian revival took place during the 1930s but this was mainly confined to cinema architecture and had much more to do with Cecil B. de Mille than Napoleon.)

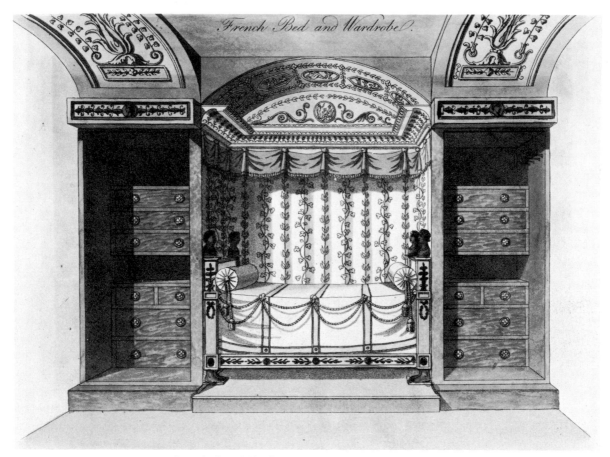

French Bed and Wardrobe.

70   *Design for a bed with 'built-in' wardrobes (see p. 145). The bed-ends are Nubian versions of the more usual Egyptian figures. From Smith's* A Collection of Designs for Household Furniture and Decoration, *1808*

Animal forms based on the lion are also associated with furniture in the Egyptian style, heads being found as arm terminals and applied ornamental detail, paw-like feet on chairs, sofas, tables and so on (they tend to be especially huge and hairy on those tables which are supported on central columns). Many Regency chair legs are in fact entirely in the form of an animal's back leg, and this form too was adopted from Egyptian furniture, as may be seen by studying existing examples of Egyptian chairs and stools preserved in museum collections.

But we have also to reckon with another source for this type of decoration. In 1807 there appeared a book of designs entitled *Household Furniture and Decoration* by Thomas Hope (?1770–1831), and the furniture in question was that which he had designed for his own house, also planned and built by himself. Hope was a rich and talented connoisseur and a gifted amateur archaeologist, who had studied at first hand the ancient civilisations not only of Greece but of Egypt,

71 *One of the apartments in Thomas Hope's London house (Duchess Street), about 1808. In this re-creation of a Greek temple the shrine-like object at the far end is a chamber organ*

Turkey and Syria as well. As a result of these studies his furniture designs were the first in this country to reflect consistently the influence of accurate archaeological knowledge based on first-hand study and excavation of lesser-known sites.

In 1805 Hope created a curious house in Surrey, The Deepdene, now demolished. The interiors of this mansion, and of his London residence in Duchess Street, showed the extent of his learning in Greek and other architectural styles as well as providing a fit setting for his large collection of antiquities and for the furniture which he designed *en suite*. A typical Hope piece, later much copied, is the 'lion monopodium stand', a small round table resting on three legs, each of which is composed of a curious creature made up from a lion's head attached to a lion-like back leg (monopodium = one support). These lion monopodia (though, to do him justice, Hope himself refers to the creature as a chimera, a mythical beast) figure prominently on much furniture

72   *Lion monopodium tripod stand. A similar one can be seen in the right-hand corner of the Duchess Street interior. (V. and A. Museum)*

of the period, acting as the supports for sideboards and a variety of tables, chairs and sofas. The creature itself was not of course invented by Hope but merely adapted by him from classical precedents. (There is a fine set of black-and-gold painted furniture designed by Hope at Buscot Park in Oxfordshire.)

Hope's brand of Greek classicism is a good deal more severe than anything that had preceded it during the eighteenth century. Something of this approach is foreshadowed by Sheraton in the two works published after his original famous pattern book. These were the *Cabinet Dictionary* of 1803 and an unfinished *Encyclopaedia* of 1804–06 whose erratic style faithfully reflects its author's approaching insanity. Nevertheless, in these two works Sheraton showed, for the first time in any published designs, a determination to create classical pieces of a new simplicity, purged of excessive and unsuitable ornament, and based on genuine precedents. This late interest in an authentic antiquity is shown, for example, in the 1803 *Dictionary* by his inclusion of two designs for what he calls 'herculaneums'; these are simply armchairs modelled on those found in stone and bronze, or represented in painting, at Herculaneum and Pompeii. This was an approach of which Hope would entirely have approved, for he himself developed a type of chair copied from a Greek example known as the klismos and first shown in sculptures of the sixth century B.C. This chair – hard, wide and deep, with concave back often resting on a single support – was widely copied throughout Europe, and was still influential at the beginning of the Victorian era. From it was originally adapted that style of leg which came a little later to be associated with the sabre shape.

The severity of Hope's Grecian-style architecture was not peculiar to himself but was in tune with a general movement towards building entirely in the Greek classical manner, freed from all the decorative elements that had derived from the Romans. The enthusiasm for this, which paralleled the Gothic and the picturesque though never perhaps reaching the same level of popularity, began about 1804 and continued until the 1830s. It was stimulated especially by two events, (1) the purchase in 1816, by public subscription, of the sculptured reliefs brought by Lord Elgin from the Parthenon at Athens, and (2) the Greek revolt against the Turks in 1821, in which the ultra-Romantic figure of Lord Byron took part and during which he died (though from sickness, not wounds). When all this has been said, however, it is still true to claim that much of the impetus for the revival of pure Greek classicism did in fact come from the work and writings of Hope.

The Greek classical style was thought to be especially suitable for large public buildings, such as the National Gallery (by William Wilkins, begun 1833) and the British Museum (by Robert Smirke, built 1823–47), the latter distinguished by its gigantic portico and colonnade. However, many houses throughout the country were also built in the style, which is perhaps best described as being something akin to Palladianism but shorn of much ornamental detail,

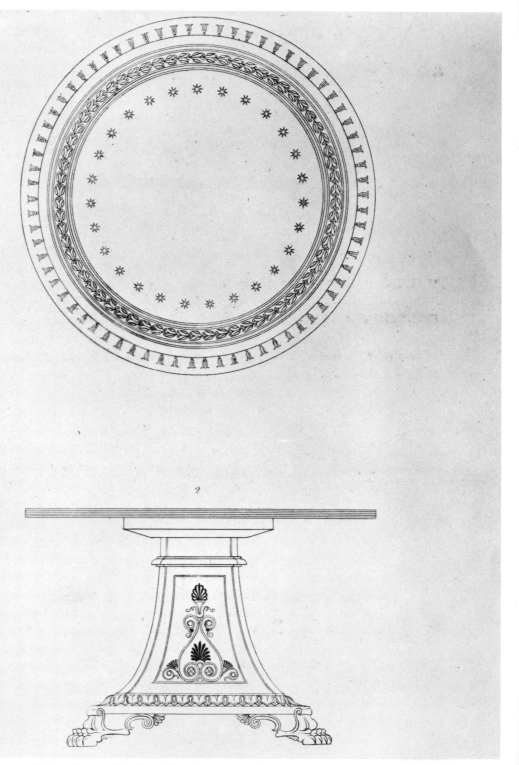

73 *Design for a table, from Hope's* Household Furniture and Decoration, *1807*

74 *Table closely based on Hope's design though without the decorations on the central pillar. Mahogany, with ornament in ebony and silver*

both inside and out. Surfaces are broad and flat, the Corinthian column with its foliated capital is seldom used, and a specifically Greek type of pediment with vertical wing-like projections at the corners was introduced and was used also on bookcases, bureaux, wardrobes, etc. Books of designs for Greek-style houses were issued in exactly the same way as those for the picturesque villas, though not in such numbers. A good example of the smaller Greek classical country house is Philipps House near Dinton in Wiltshire, built between 1805 and 1815 by James Wyatt's nephew Sir Jeffrey Wyatville. Melford Hall, (Suffolk), a Tudor house, has a remodelled Regency interior in the Greek manner.

Midway between the picturesque and the severely classical stands the very individual work of the architect John Soane (1753–1837). In 1788 Soane was appointed Surveyor to the Bank of England, a post which gained him social status, financial security and an eventual knighthood. Much of his subsequent professional life was spent in redesigning and rebuilding the Bank, but he also found time to design houses in a classical but highly personal style, characterised by such features as very wide-span arches, blind niches instead of windows, and cunning lighting by means of shallow domes which also replace windows. Unfortunately few of his houses remain exactly as he built them, but enough still exists to testify to his individuality. Shotesham (Norfolk) and Pitzhanger Manor (Middlesex), now Ealing Central Library, are good representative exteriors. The main façade of Shotesham, faced with pale yellow brick, reveals three storeys with a shallow central gable and six Ionic pilasters rising through the first two storeys. The general impression is of flatness, even monotony. Pitzhanger, on the other hand, which Soane built for himself, has an imposing and lively façade (again in brick) whose chief feature consists of four free-standing Ionic columns topped by classical figures. Soane favoured round-headed windows, or flat-headed ones set in shallow arches.

There are good Soane interiors still to be seen at a number of country houses, for example Aynhoe Park (Northamptonshire), where the library, drawing room and vestibule all display the typical wide, shallow arch and round-headed niches. The dome of the vestibule is of a low, umbrella-like shape especially favoured by Soane, and the staircase is lit by a small dome in his most typical manner. There seems to be nothing in any of this polished and rather cold-seeming work of that fanciful spirit which is associated with the picturesque. Yet a visit to Soane's London house (number 12, Lincoln's Inn Fields), a place of fascinating nooks, corners and crannies specially built and adapted to house the vast collection of priceless paintings, curios and valuables which he eventually left to the nation, is a useful antidote to any impression of Soane as a clinically formal and severe architect; moreover there exist designs which show that he could be as fancifully picturesque as Nash when he chose.

The name of Nash and the theme of the picturesque lead us inevitably to Brighton. The Prince Regent's romance with Brighthelmstone (as the original

75 *Chair of ebonised wood, carved and gilded, about 1810. The cushion is a modern replacement. (V. and A. Museum)*

fishing village was called) began in 1783, when he first went there to try what
the newly fashionable fad of sea-bathing could do for his various ailments. In
1786 he commissioned the architect Henry Holland to create for him a villa
known as the Marine Pavilion, basically a low, two-storey building consisting
of two wings and a central circular domed area. Some of Holland's interiors
were designed in the fanciful Chinese style that was now beginning to have
something of a revival. Indeed at one time the Regent had considered whether
perhaps the whole of the Pavilion could be enlarged and remodelled throughout 'à la Chinois', but in the end, he was persuaded that a Hindu rather than a
Chinese style would be more suitable for the exterior of any new version of the
Pavilion. India had begun to exert a great fascination on Regency thought,
linking up especially with the movement towards the romantic, the exotic
and the picturesque that found its supreme literary expression in Coleridge's
mysterious dream of Kubla Khan's 'stately pleasure dome'. Indeed this famous
poem (composed in 1797) may well have played some part in the creation of
that rather more solid and tangible pleasure dome in the beautiful yet prosaic
setting of seaside Sussex. But more importantly, there already existed (and still
does) in Gloucestershire a house built in the Indian style for a retired East
India Company official; this house, Sezincote, was modelled directly on drawings made in India. It is certainly no accident that the Royal Stables at Brighton
(now known as the Dome and converted into a theatre-cum-concert hall) very
closely resemble parts of Sezincote.

The final well-known façade of the Pavilion we owe of course to John Nash,
appointed Surveyor-General in 1815 and beginning his 'improvements' (cost-
ing eventually some £148,000) at Brighton in the same year. Yet behind the
exoticism of the garden front with its onion domes, minarets and Moorish
arches can still be traced the basic outlines of Henry Holland's much more
modest house, and while one cannot fail to be impressed by the opulent
magnificence of Nash's pseudo-Oriental interior decorations, it is still the
revived Chinese style originally initiated by Holland that most consistently
impresses itself on the visitor. This is encountered almost at once, in the
Gallery immediately behind the Entrance Hall, where the original mainly
pink-and-gold colours have recently been restored after overpainting in 1877,
and where the well-known ingredients of dragons, trellis, mandarins, bells and
pagodas greet the visitor. Imitation bamboo, amazingly well simulated in
painted cast iron, forms the balustrades of the two double staircases which lead
up to the first floor from each end of the Gallery, and in 1821 George IV's
recently completed bedroom was equipped with a suite of furniture in beechwood again cleverly turned to resemble bamboo.

However, this time the Chinese style failed to catch the public fancy to the
extent it had done during the eighteenth century. The Prince Regent himself
hinted later that he had encouraged it, together with the Hindu style, as an
antidote to the French influence which, although he preferred, he could not be

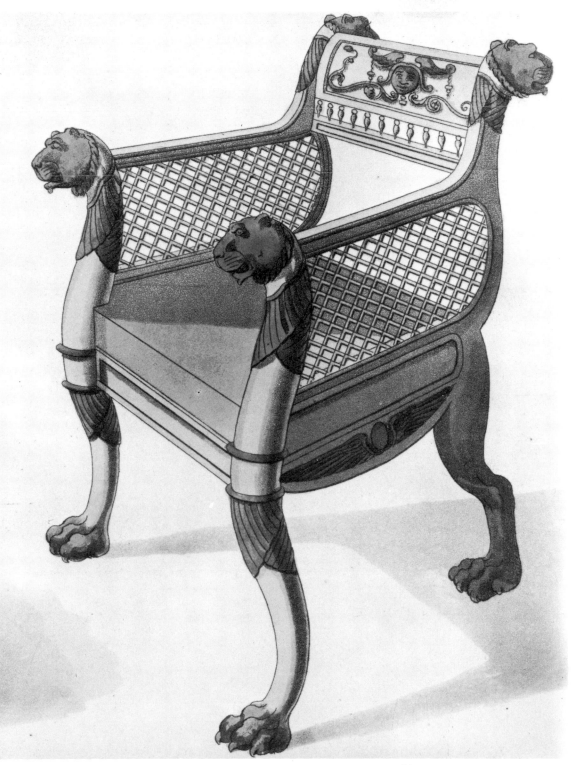

76   *Design for a chair, from Smith's* A Collection of Designs for Household Furniture and Decoration, 1808. *This may well have been the source of inspiration for the chair in the preceding illustration*

seen to encourage at a time when our relations with France were strained. Even if this was the truth, many of his subjects looked on his Oriental cavortings with undisguised contempt, and a variety of rude and insulting caricatures appeared which lampooned him in the character of a grossly fat mandarin. A contemporary satirist invited his readers to view the Pavilion, 'Where neither genius, taste nor fancy dwells:/Monkeys, mandarins, a motley crew,/Bridges, pagodas, swings and tinkling bells.' And while not everyone was ready to be quite so disparaging, and some were even prepared to make use of the Chinese style themselves, it was not used with quite the same zest as during its mid-eighteenth-century heyday.

In fact a new note of caution can be detected in the few Chinese-style designs that were actually published at this time. For example, in a pattern book of 1808 we find an idea for the end wall of a Chinese drawing room, in which the chimneypiece, disguised as a pagoda, is surmounted by plate glass to which is stuck carved wooden foliage and flanked at each side by recesses painted with landscapes. The caption informs us, in a slightly threatening tone, that 'The good effect of this design will depend much on the taste of the parties super-

77 *Regency Gothic chair, about 1810, and dining room chair, about 1825–30*

intending its execution, who should be well versed in the Chinese style, and avoid introducing any species of ornament and arrangement not in accordance with this peculiar taste.'

This is an attitude which the eighteenth century would not have understood at all. Nor would it have appreciated another remark from the same book, this time concerning the Gothic style: 'Great care should be taken . . . to adopt a uniformity of ornament, and not to introduce any mélange of dates and styles.' Strawberry Hill is the most notable mélange of dates and styles of its kind in existence. These statements show that a more serious and consciously scholarly attitude towards the lighter forms of architecture and decoration was in being long before the Victorian era with which it is usually associated.

The book from which these quotations are taken was almost the last important contribution to the great series of furniture pattern books. Entitled *A Collection of Designs for Household Furniture and Decoration*, it was published in 1808 by George Smith who, like Chippendale and Hepplewhite, was a practising cabinet-maker. Just as Robert Adam's style in furniture had been made more accessible through the work of Hepplewhite, so Thomas Hope's ideas reached a wider public via the designs of Smith. In addition to Hope's archaeological and classical influence, however, the plates in Smith's book show all the additional ingredients which make Regency furniture so fascinating – the Egyptian, the Gothic, the Chinese, the militaristic. Most of his designs tend to be overloaded with ornament, but he continued Hepplewhite's tradition of providing useful, practical pieces for the bedroom and dressing room. His is the design for built-in furniture mentioned on p. 145, and in one idea for a wardrobe we are told that the dresses are 'to be suspended on arms sliding on an iron rod', a method still used in some modern wardrobes today. The idea of hanging clothes up at all was still fairly new; during most of the eighteenth century the prevailing custom had been to fold them away in drawers or on shelves.

In 1826 Smith produced a second book of designs, *The Cabinet Maker and Upholsterer's Guide*, the whole tone and content of which is markedly different from his earlier collection. Although the designs seem at first sight to be considerably more simple than those of 1808, it soon becomes obvious that this is a simplicity born of a desperate lack of inspiration, and in fact the book reflects only too clearly what has been called 'the impending bankruptcy of taste in England'.* It abounds in such things as ugly, lumpy sideboards, heavy sofas balanced on spindly carved legs with insubstantial castors, chairs whose fussy design and ill-conceived decoration (a hopeless mish-mash of the old traditional motifs) contain the seeds of utter decay. Smith, obviously feeling the need to apologise, blames 'the necessity for economy urged by so many at the present day' (familiar words!), and also dismisses his own earlier book as 'rendered obsolete and inapplicable . . . by the change of taste and rapid improvements' of

*R. Fastnedge, *English furniture styles from 1500 to 1830*, p. 275. 1964.

the intervening 20 years. All this gives further point to the undoubted fact that the decline in standards of furniture design, which we tend to associate mainly with the Victorians, in fact set in rather more than a decade earlier. A heavy price was about to be paid for all the past achievements in the design, style and construction of furniture.

CHAPTER SEVEN

Victorian Extravagance

*W*HEN in 1837 the 18-year-old Victoria ascended the British throne, no immediate and drastic changes in artistic styles took place. But there was an intensification of changes which – as shown in the preceding chapter – had already begun to manifest themselves some years previously, and the style most obviously affected was the Gothic. From the original frivolous fantasies of Strawberry Hill the Victorian version of Gothic became not only on the whole more scholarly but above all religious in both tone and content.*

This introduction of a religious note may be largely attributed to the influence of A. W. N. Pugin (1812–1852). The son of one of John Nash's draughtsmen, himself deeply interested in the style, the sensitive yet incredibly energetic Pugin came early to the conclusion that original Gothic architecture was fundamentally religious and specifically Christian, the medieval workman's expression of his faith. Thus in the eyes of Pugin (who himself was strongly religious, adopted Roman Catholicism, and found all details of ritual and ceremonial entirely absorbing), Gothic was inevitably the best and purest form of architecture. No building, he considered, could be termed truly Christian in intent or inspiration unless it had somewhere about it the pointed arch associated with medieval architecture at its highest pitch of development. To him a Gothic building announced its purpose clearly and unambiguously, and was honestly built of materials that were allowed to be themselves, so that wood looked like wood, stone like stone, and so forth.

Once again it was through the medium of a book that important artistic ideas were to be communicated effectively to a wider public. In 1836 Pugin published a work called *Contrasts* in which he compared and contrasted medieval buildings with their nineteenth-century equivalents, to the undoubted detriment of the latter. The book made considerable impact on public opinion; years later, so did Pugin's design and furnishing of a corner called the 'Medieval Court' at the 1851 Great Exhibition, in which items intended mainly for religious use were shown. His buildings were less generally influential. As a Roman Catholic

*Some of the best and most consistent examples of Victorian Gothic are to be found in vicarages and – more surprisingly – country railway stations.

architect working at a time when his faith was viewed with deep suspicion, his best hope lay in discovering rich patrons of the same religious persuasion, but he managed to find only two rich enough to finance his schemes, which were always grandiose. For Charles Scarisbrick, an eccentric bachelor mostly unseen even by his own servants, Pugin built Scarisbrick Hall in a wild and marshy part of Lancashire. Scarisbrick is a rambling Fonthill-type mansion dominated by a tall spire and containing panelled and gilded apartments such as a lofty Banqueting Hall (wasted, one feels, on the original owner), an Oak Room, and a Tudor Room which serves as a reminder that the nucleus of the house was the original 1595 west wing which Pugin incorporated into his design. For the Earl of Shrewsbury Pugin built another huge mansion, Alton Towers, complete with a chapel as large as a smallish church; Lord Shrewsbury also put up the money for a number of new Roman Catholic churches designed by Pugin including the cathedral of St Chad in Birmingham. Pugin's churches are lofty and rich with colour, though since the available funds had to be carefully allocated this richness is mostly confined to the chancels and sanctuaries.

There is, however, one area of Pugin's work which is of national importance. When in 1835 the architect Charles Barry won the competition to build the Houses of Parliament as a replacement for the old Palace of Westminster, burnt down in 1834, he selected Pugin to provide the decorative details, though he himself had conceived the overall plan and design and continued to oversee the entire project. The wealth of pseudo-medieval carving and panelling, both inside and out the great complex of buildings, represents Pugin at his finest and most inspired and cannot fail to have influenced his contemporaries in the creation of Gothic house interiors.

His theories and workmanship as applied specifically to furniture were publicised in another book, *Gothic Furniture in the Style of the Fifteenth Century* (1835). The plates show a welcome return to true medieval forms and decoration. The comparative restraint of these designs and of such pieces of Pugin's furniture as have actually survived is due to his belief that decoration is not something to be applied externally and haphazardly entirely for its own sake, but should grow naturally out of the basic form which it ornaments. It was not Pugin's fault if most of those who aspired to imitate him failed entirely to learn this lesson.

'What passes for Gothic furniture among cabinet-makers and upholsterers is, generally, a very different thing from the correct Gothic designs supplied by architects who have imbued their minds with this style of art.' (J. C. Loudon, *An Encyclopaedia of Cottage, Farm and Villa Architecture and Furniture*, 1833.)

It is significant that the competition for the new Houses of Parliament was the first occasion on which the Gothic style was specifically laid down for an

78 *Scarisbrick Hall, Lancashire. By A. W. N. Pugin, 1837–1845. The irregular façade and soaring tower are reminiscent of Fonthill Abbey*

official Government building. (When, some years later, Gilbert Scott wanted to use Gothic for the new Foreign Office he was not allowed to do so and had to revert to a classical style. What the Foreign Office might have looked like may be gathered from Scott's St Pancras Station, a grand pinnacled extravaganza in high-flown Gothic.) It is also significant that the proposed alternative to Gothic in the terms of the competition was the so-called 'Elizabethan' style, for though this can be traced back to the late 1820s and especially to Scott's novel *Kenilworth* (1821), it also continued to be popular throughout much of the Victorian era. Since it combined elements of both the Elizabethan and Jacobean styles a more suitable name might be 'Jacobethan'. Representative houses in the style are Highclere Castle, Hampshire (Charles Barry, 1840), Thoresby Hall, Nottinghamshire (1864) and Harlaxton Manor, Lincolnshire (begun 1831; both these houses by Anthony Salvin). Just as the prodigy houses of the late Tudor and early Stuart eras had reflected the self-confidence of a new ruling class, so the Jacobethan houses of the Victorians reflected the self-confidence of a new race of self-made men – manufacturers and merchant princes, nouveaux riches who had got where they were by hard work and a good head for business in an increasingly commercial world, and wanted everyone to know it.

Behind these houses may be detected the influence – in greater or lesser degree, in isolation or in glorious hotch-potch – of Hardwick, Longleat, Wollaton, Burghley and a dozen or so more of famous old prodigy houses. Indoors the Elizabethan style was considered especially appropriate to the fittings and furnishings of such apartments as entrance halls, billiards rooms, dining rooms and libraries, and a certain amount of furniture was designed in keeping with it. Most typical are the chairs, many with high backs incorporating barley sugar twist columns not in fact seen in genuine chairs before the seventeenth century; often these backs were inappropriately covered with padded upholstery or panels of Berlin woolwork. Furniture in the Jacobethan style was not infrequently made of pieces of original woodwork ('cannibalised'

79   *Harlaxton Manor, Lincolnshire. By Anthony Salvin, 1830s. Victorian Jacobethan at its most magnificent and (almost) convincing*

chairs, etc.) assembled together; J. C. Loudon remarks that 'There are abundant remains of every kind of Elizabethan furniture to be purchased of collectors. These, when in fragments, are put together, and made up into every article of furniture now in use.'

The Victorians also favoured an Italian style, based for the most part loosely on Italian Renaissance palazzi and villas. The style received an important boost from the building in 1846 of Osborne House, designed by Prince Albert as an Isle of Wight retreat for himself, the Queen and their family. It has Italianate towers, unusually large windows (for Victorian England), and a loggia on the first floor, and was especially built where it stands because the view and coastline reminded Albert of the Bay of Naples. Schemes of interior decoration were devised to suit Italian-style houses, and with earnest Victorian scholarship these were usually based on the High Renaissance style developed by the school of Raphael. But on the whole the style was used less for private houses than for public buildings, such as the quadrangle of the Victoria and Albert Museum (about 1868).

The diversity and mixture of architectural styles and decoration that make

80 *Osborne House, Isle of Wight. By Prince Albert and Thomas Cubitt, 1848. An Italian palazzo in a slice of Hampshire*

up the Victorian house ensure that visits to previously unknown houses of the period are something of an adventure. One never knows quite what to expect. It is certain, however, that the plan of all but the smallest house is likely to be fairly complicated. The reasons for this were not architectural but social. In an age notorious for its wide range of domestic taboos, etiquette required that the social divisions between the members of a family, their guests and servants, should be physically enforceable by means of separate entrances, stairways and passages, and this need for segregation posed a major problem for many an architect. Never before had the back stairs or the green-baize door separating servants' quarters from the house proper loomed so large in importance.

The entrance halls of Victorian houses, like those of Robert Adam in an earlier age, were designed to impress. High, usually gloomy, and often paved with coloured encaustic tiles based on medieval patterns and manufactured by Messrs Minton or Messrs May and Company, they were hung round with darkly-varnished pictures and with weapons and trophies of the chase, and the effect of all this was not lost on those whose incomes and houses were both on a smaller scale. 'I bought a pair of stag's heads made of plaster-of-Paris and coloured brown. They will look just the thing for our little hall, and give it style; the heads are excellent imitations.'* Gothic, so closely linked with baronial magnificence, was especially favoured for entrance halls, as also for the heavy staircases which rose up out of them. Jacobethan was also popular here, not only for the hall and stairs themselves but also for such pieces of furniture as the hall-stand (unknown before about 1830), a flat-backed post with peg-strewn branches and a console table attachment, especially useful in the narrower and more passage-like entrance halls of town houses.

From the hall to the dining room is usually only a short distance. Dining tables were now of two distinct types. In smaller households round tables on heavy tripod supports were popular, having derived from the Regency 'loo' table originally developed for the card game of that name (in fact many such tables actually were loo tables, only their function having changed over the years). Larger households favoured a rectangular type standing on four dropsical turned legs; this could be extended by the insertion of extra leaves in the centre. Such tables were often accompanied by sets of square-backed, leather-upholstered dining chairs in the debased classical style of the late Regency, some of them showing a new feature of construction in that the top rail is T-shaped and is fitted onto the tops of the uprights with its ends jutting out beyond them. It was not long before even the commonest of kitchen chairs were

*G. and W. Grossmith, *The Diary of a Nobody*, p. 68, 1946 ed. (first published 1894). In 1873 the Rev. Francis Kilvert records an improvement on this: visiting Draycot House near Chippenham, Wiltshire, he found that in the entrance hall, 'The walls were ornamented with fallow bucks' heads and horns, from every branch tip of which sprung a jet of gas.' (*Kilvert's Diary, 1870–1879*, p. 231, 1974 ed. in Jonathan Cape Paperbacks.)

sharing this feature.

But the dining room was dominated by the sideboard, which by the late 1840s had become a solid monstrosity of heavily over-carved, over-decorated mahogany or rosewood, its upper back acting as a frame for great sheets of mirror glass whose main purpose was to reflect the family plate and help to make everything look twice as opulent as it really was. (Some truly horrific examples appeared at the 1851 Great Exhibition.) Again the Jacobethan was a favourite style. Popular too from the 1850s onwards were the solid oak sideboards carved overall in a naturalistic style initiated by Messrs Cooke of Warwick, of which the most famous example is the Kenilworth Buffet in Warwick Castle. Here scenes from Sir Walter Scott's novel *Kenilworth* (his romanticised version of events at the court of Queen Elizabeth I) are translated into terms of wood-carving of great technical skill but doubtful artistic value. A similar sideboard in the Victoria and Albert Museum tells the story of Robinson Crusoe. It is hard to see what any of this had to do with the business of eating and drinking. More obviously appropriate were those sideboards whose panels were merely carved with naturalistic dead game, bunches of grapes and so on, all in high relief.

Huge, solid pieces of this type were especially appropriate to the room in which huge, solid meals were consumed daily and where, above all, the solemn ritual of the dinner party was regularly enacted. Even the table furnishings were designed in keeping. 'Hideous solidity was the characteristic of the Podsnap plate. Everything was made to look as heavy as it could, and to take up as much room as possible.' * Central to the Podsnap dinner table was 'a corpulent straddling épergne [table centre], blotched all over as if it had broken out into an eruption rather than been ornamented'; this was flanked by 'four silver wine coolers, each furnished with four staring heads, each head obtrusively carrying a big silver ring in each of its ears' – a fictional account, but none the less entirely true to life.

The dining room was not only used for eating. Sometimes it was the regular setting for another typically Victorian ritual, that of family prayers. 'The urns are hissing, the plate is shining; the father of the house, standing up, reads from a gilt book for three or four minutes in a measured cadence. The members of the family are around the table in an attitude of decent reverence, the younger children whisper responses at their mother's knees; the governess worships a little apart; the maids and the large footmen are in a cluster before their chairs, the upper servants performing their devotion on the other side of the sideboard; the nurse whisks about the unconscious last-born and tosses it up and down during the ceremony.' † The universal custom of family prayers led to the introduction of that curious piece of furniture, the prie-Dieu chair. As a chair, its extremely low seat and long, narrow T-shaped back made it impractical;

*C. Dickens, *Our Mutual Friend*, chap. XI.   †W. M. Thackeray, *The Newcomes*, chap. XIV.

however, when turned around and knelt on, the seat being used as a hassock and the T-shaped back as an elbow rest, its true *raison d'être* becomes immediately obvious. Its style was usually Jacobethan, the upholstery – including a panel down the centre of the back – often consisting of embroidery or Berlin wool-work (needlework based on squared paper patterns originally introduced from Berlin in about 1805).

In addition to the dining room, the main rooms on the ground floor might include a library – of all rooms, the least changed in appearance and furnishings since the previous century – a billiards room, and a parlour and/or morning room used for everyday living (the saloon or drawing room being reserved for special occasions only). Attached to the house, and forming a sort of indoor garden extension to it, there might also be a conservatory. Sir Osbert Lancaster has described the conservatory at his grandfather's house on Putney Hill as being 'always steeped in a curious, jungle romance. Around a tiled pool, in which two depressed golden carp of immense size circulated among improbable conch-shells, there flourished palms and giant ferns and banks of potted lobelias and calceolarias beneath a glazed sky barely visible through a tangle of maiden-hair.'* Conservatories owed their popularity to a general interest in the collection of rare and unusual plants (stimulated by the rapid expansion of the Empire), combined with the impact of the new cast iron and glass architecture as exemplified above all by Joseph Paxton's Great Conservatory at Chatsworth (completed 1841). Second only to it in size, and probably surpassing it in beauty and atmosphere (though a comparison is no longer possible, since the Chatsworth Conservatory has been demolished) is the two-storey-high conservatory at Flintham near Newark. This is a true winter garden, such as that described by the Victorian novelist C. M. Yonge as 'a fairy land, where no care or grief or weariness could come' (*The Daisy Chain*, 1856).

The main reception room, though it might be on the ground floor, was also not infrequently situated on the first floor, the grand staircase making a suitably impressive approach to it. This was especially true of town houses. Mr Dumps, the hero of one of Dickens's *Sketches by Boz*, arrives at a christening party and is ushered upstairs: 'There was a great smell of nutmeg, port wine and almonds on the staircase; the covers were taken off the stair-carpet; and the figure of Venus on the first landing looked as if she were ashamed of the composition candle in her right hand. . . . The female servant ushered Dumps into a front drawing room, very prettily furnished, with a plentiful sprinkling of little baskets, paper table mats, china watchmen, pink and gold albums, and rainbow-bound little books on the tables.' In a very few words (though actually writing in the immediate pre-Victorian era) Dickens manages here to convey a sense of that meaningless clutter which was such a feature of Victorian rooms, whether in the houses of the rich or (as in this case) the not-so-rich. This clutter, so alien

* *All done from memory*, p. 58. 1963.

81 *'Elizabethan' chair of carved and turned mahogany, with seat and back panel of
tent-stitched embroidery, about 1845. (V. and A. Museum)*

to our modern conception of daily living, was in fact nothing less than a parade of wordly goods whose extent and profusion were taken as an indication of wealth and social status. Prints and paintings cluttered the walls, knick-knacks of every description cluttered tables and mantelpieces, and furniture cluttered the rooms.

Another contemporary description is offered by J. C. Loudon, who writes:

A large round table is usually placed in the middle of the drawing-room, on which are generally books of prints and other things to amuse the company. . . . Two card tables would stand one on each side of the fireplace: and, besides all these, we must have tables of various sizes, some small ones on pillars; a chess table, with an inlaid marble top, the men placed upon it; a large china dish set in a gilt sort of tripod; a sort of table flower-stand; and I cannot tell what besides. . . . Writing, work, and drawing boxes of handsome kinds, and everything amusing, curious, or ornamental, is in its place in the drawing-room; but the host of trumpery toys so often seen there would be unworthy of a place in a room like this. . . . There should be nothing superfluous.

The final comment takes one's breath away.

'There were too many chairs', decides Sylvia (in V. Sackville West's novel *The Edwardians*), surveying with some distaste a 'society' drawing room of about 1905, 'Too many hassocks, too many small tables, too much pampas grass in crane-necked vases, too many blinds and curtains looped and festooned about the windows. The whole effect was fusty, musty, and dusty. . . . Everything had something else superimposed upon it; the overmantel bore its load of ornaments on each bracket, the mantel-shelf itself was decked with a strip of damask heavily fringed, the piano was covered over by a square of Damascus velvet, on which more photographs and more ornaments were insecurely balanced.'

Thus the drawing room, the decoration of which was frequently in the white-and-gold Rococo style incorrectly known as 'Louis Quatorze' (as at Belvoir Castle), was no less over-filled than the other rooms, except on those occasions when the carpet was rolled back and a ball took place. To the music of an instrumental group, or perhaps a single pianist according to the means of the family, the younger guests revolved in an endless succession of waltzes while the chaperones looked on. Many households owned two pianos, an upright in the schoolroom and a grand in the drawing room. Originally the shape of the grand piano had been very much like that of the harpsichord, and during the late eighteenth and early nineteenth centuries the two co-existed happily enough. But, gradually, changing styles and tastes in music meant that the harpsichord (which is *not* related to the piano except very superficially) dropped out of favour and use, while the grand piano became ever larger and heavier, its case encrusted with carving and metal mounts, its bulbous legs swollen with the tremendous weight they were expected to support (the interior frame now being of iron instead of wood). For a time some Victorian households retained an oblong form of piano known illogically as a 'square' piano and popular during the Regency era, but by the 1850s the monstrous grand reigned supreme in every fashionable drawing room. The schoolroom upright, on the other hand, was likely to be pre-1830s, tall and shallow, with the frame above the keyboard fronted with a panel of pleated red silk, although highly ornamental uprights for drawing room use were also made.

Although the stigma is not entirely deserved, it is certainly true that heaviness and over-ornamentation are the main features which most people associate with Victorian furniture in general. As regards seat furniture in particular, however, it is surely the extraordinary interest in sheer bodily comfort that must strike one most forcibly. To this we owe the enormous amount of padding and upholstery that is characteristic of the period, plush being the most common material and the coiled spring being 'in' by the 1840s. The same interest was responsible for the proliferation of many different types of easy chairs, sofas, settees and couches, and even for the development of new forms such as the two- or three-seater 'sociable' designed on an S-shaped plan to encourage relaxed conversation between the sexes without any danger of unseemly physical contact. The legs of many such pieces were completely concealed under long heavy fringes, a custom in which (together with the alleged draping of piano legs) some experts have professed to detect psychological implications of a sexual nature. Much of the upholstery was held in place by the deep buttoning which is characteristic of the period and was certainly one of the best dirt-traps ever invented.

Only one entirely novel shape of chair was produced during the Victorian era. This was the famous 'balloon-back' whose origins, like those of so much Victorian furniture in general, are to be found in the designs of the later Regency. The balloon-back, which is open, is characterised by the pinching-in of the back uprights at the bar or cross-rail which runs across the back near its centre, with the consequent bulging out of the back above it. This shape was fully established by the 1850s and on the whole balloon-back chairs manage to avoid over-ornamentation, though the front legs and cross-rail may be carved. In addition the front legs are usually turned, though the back ones remain plain and slightly splayed, but more elegant models may have cabriole legs in a French Rococo style specially intended to chime in with 'Louis Quatorze' decorations.

French influence of a different type began to make itself felt in the furniture of the 1870s and '80s. This was part of a general Continental influence beginning in the 1860s and in some measure due to the influence of the various exhibitions that took place all over Europe in the wake of the Great Exhibition of 1851 (discussed below). Perhaps the most marked instance of this was the revived interest in boulle, this time a much more serious affair than the mild flirtation indulged in during the Regency (see p. 143). Architecturally, French influence at this time is reflected in the imitation châteaux such as Waddesdon Manor (Buckinghamshire) or the Bowes Museum at Barnard Castle, Durham. We ought not to forget the strong ties that existed between the courts of Victoria and of the Emperor Napoleon III, who with his Empress Eugénie sought and found permanent refuge here after his final flight from France (1871).

In the 1860s there came also a return to eighteenth-century taste, which the earlier Victorians had dismissed as barbarous. This began with an Adam revival which took its cue from a single large cabinet (now in the Victoria and Albert Museum) made by an English firm and shown at the Paris Exhibition of 1855. Within ten years extremely accurate copies, as well as inaccurate adaptations, of genuine Chippendale, Hepplewhite and Sheraton pieces were being widely produced, and even today these sometimes have the power to deceive experts as to their true date of origin. However, they ought not to be regarded just as fakes but as fine pieces of furniture in their own right.

An important feature of Victorian furniture is the uninhibited use of all sorts of new materials. This had been done before, notably by the Adam brothers, but never to such an extent, and the Victorians moreover had the additional advantages of greatly improved and expanded industrial processes. One obvious result of this is their widespread use of cast iron, especially for chairs, tables and benches intended for garden or conservatory use and cast in shapes passably imitating tree trunks, roots and so on. Hollow iron tubing was used for the frames of beds and rocking chairs from the 1840s on. But to our minds perhaps the most curious material to enjoy considerable vogue in the mid-century was papier-mâché, of which the Birmingham firm of Jennens and Bettridge had a virtual monopoly (they filled an entire stand with it at the 1851 Exhibition). Known already by the 1770s though not at that time popular, this technique of baking sized and moulded sheets of paper to a rock-like consistency was found to lend itself to a wide variety of objects ranging from tea trays to bed-heads, chairs, and even a piano case (though it was found advisable to construct larger items of furniture over iron frames). The main surface was normally lacquered black and ornamented with paints, enamels, gold dust and mother-of-pearl.

The brass bedstead first appeared in Victorian bedrooms about 1850, and became so popular that it immediately proclaims itself even when partly concealed by drapery and other embellishments such as the papier-mâché bed-ends mentioned above. The more elaborate examples were fitted with a half-tester which now enjoyed a period of renewed popularity. However, the traditional 'four-poster' or full tester was still made in wood and usually showing the influence of the Gothic or Jacobethan tastes. In more simple households the draping of beds in Regency fashion long continued popular.

Bedrooms were no less full of furniture and knick-knacks than the reception rooms, and much space was taken up by massive mahogany wardrobes with

82 *Chair of papier-mâché inlaid with mother-of-pearl, about 1850. (V. and A. Museum)*

frowning cornices and inset plate glass mirrors which had replaced the elegant cheval mirrors of the late eighteenth century and Regency periods. In all bed-rooms stood the washstand with marble top, jug and basin, and slop-pail beneath, hot water being brought up to the rooms in brass cans or large jugs. For more extensive washing the hip-bath was mainly used, again having to be filled and emptied by hand. The idea of allotting a separate room in which to bathe took hold gradually, until as the century neared its close bathrooms with piped water as we know them became relatively common, the baths themselves either standing isolated on enormous paw feet or enclosed in heavy wooden surrounds with control panels that bristle with porcelain-headed brass knobs reminiscent of organ stops.

Similarly, the water closet as we know it today was a product of the later nineteenth century, although first patented in 1775. Kent provided for one off the entrance hall at Holkham, Adam for four at Luton Hoo; the actor Garrick's fashionable modern town house in the Adam brothers' Adelphi boasted three, his country house at Hampton in Middlesex only one. Through-out the earlier Victorian era there was a gradual acceptance of the water closet as a necessary adjunct to modern life, and this attitude was greatly strengthened after an official report of 1842 had firmly established the connection between bad or non-existent sanitation and diseases such as typhoid fever, cholera and dysentery. Nevertheless, for far too long in far too many smaller houses the 'privy' continued to be the norm, and was to be found among the outhouses behind the house, in the stable yard, or at the end of a garden path. Since a visit to it was not always practicable it was usefully supplemented by the chamber pot, kept in the bedside cabinet, or by the newly-arrived commode doing its best to masquerade as a stool or chair. (The word lavatory was not then used in its modern sense. Messrs Doulton's 'Improved Three-Person Tip-up Lavatory', advertised in about 1875, was not what it might seem to us but a series of three washbasins in a mahogany surround complete with mirrors.)

Special furniture evolved for nurseries – plain cupboards, high chairs, cots of wood, later with metal bars like a miniature lion's cage, and the inevitable high wiremesh fender topped by a slim brass rail. Here the head nursery maid (later to be known as the nanny) reigned supreme and parents were not welcome; indeed, through her immediate power over her charges the nanny not infre-quently held the parents also in the hollow of her hand. The nursery was her kingdom, where often she had a lesser nursery maid to help her and sometimes even a footman or pageboy assigned to her as well. Her arch-enemy was the governess, whose kingdom was the schoolroom (likewise plainly furnished) and who occupied an uncertain position in the domestic hierarchy, being neither a servant nor one of the family. She was a lonely figure (see the account of family prayers, above), whose loneliness was often increased by her being of foreign extraction, usually French or German.

Perhaps in nursery or schoolroom one might have expected to find examples of the cheap but elegant and light bentwood furniture introduced into England in the 1830s by Messrs Thonet of Vienna, and soon becoming so popular that by the end of the century its very popularity had become its undoing, since it was then considered 'common'. The graceful, steam-induced curves of bent-wood pieces (especially rocking chairs), so mercifully free of any kind of applied ornament, make for much-needed light relief from the heavy drama of most ordinary Victorian furniture. The wood itself was often ebonised or made to resemble other more expensive woods, and cane once more reappeared in the seats and backs of the chairs.

Servants, of course, could not expect to have the same kind of furniture as the gentry. The bare attic rooms in which they slept were provided with the mini-mum of items, all of them of the plainest possible description, many of them of Regency vintage, and others relegated upstairs after service on the lower floors. Some householders were genuinely interested in the welfare of their servants, an attitude which became more general towards the end of the century: a modern writer reminisces as follows: 'The big stores stocked special servants' furniture and my mother, who liked her staff to be comfortable, bought for them strong, useful stuff though unfortunately of a horrid yellow colour euphemistically called satin-wood. The lady's maid had brown furniture to mark her unique status and the governess had real visitor's furniture.'*

To take a kindly interest in one's servants was only sensible, for on them depended the smooth running of the Victorian and Edwardian home. Never before or since have so many ministered to the hourly needs of such a privileged few. (The indoor servants at Thoresby Hall numbered 50.) Yet even the servants had their own social hierarchy, with distinctions as rigid as any that governed society above stairs. Conditions and wages varied enormously from one household to another, and whilst one cannot close one's eyes to the spec-tacle of young girls toiling upstairs with heavy coal scuttles, sleeping in airless attics and working in beetle-infested, semi-subterranean kitchens and sculleries, there is at the same time no doubt that many servants of the period led what could be called quite easy lives. For example footmen, chosen primarily by their height and good physical appearance for the purpose of adding tone, seem to have had a lot of spare time on their hands and were accused (especially in *Punch* during the 1840s and '50s) of giving themselves airs well beyond their station. Cooks too were particularly privileged; not only were they virtual dictators in their own kitchens, many of them made a good private income from selling off left-overs known as 'cook's perquisites' to regular callers. The cooking itself was still done on open ranges that incorporated cast-iron ovens and hot water boilers and required daily blackleading and polishing, though by 1850 closed stoves and ovens were also becoming widely used. Kitchen furni-ture as a whole was rough and was usually dominated by a huge dresser standing

* M. Clive, *The Day of Reckoning*, p. 21. 1964.

along one wall. Sinks were of stone, with wooden draining board and surround, and single taps supplied them with cold water only. Outside the kitchen, high up on a wall near the butler's pantry, there danced and jangled the many wire-pulled bells that constantly summoned the servants to various outposts of that other world upstairs beyond the green-baize door.

The chief mirror of mid-nineteenth-century taste was the Great Exhibition of 1851. Conceived originally by Prince Albert, aided by an enthusiastic Civil Servant named Henry Cole (later the first Director of the South Kensington Museum, now the Victoria and Albert), the Great Exhibition was one of those watersheds that periodically occur in the history of a nation's artistic, industrial and social progress. It was also one of the most significant events of the whole Victorian era, coming conveniently at the very centre of the century, and expressing in a unique and powerful way the spirit of the nation at that time. The pioneering spirit of invention and enthusiasm for which the mid-Victorian period is justly famed was spectacularly liberated by the Exhibition, not least in the very building itself, the famous Crystal Palace (as *Punch* soon dubbed it).

83   *Lanhydrock House, Cornwall. Seventeenth-century but largely rebuilt in 1881 after a fire. The kitchen, complete with spits and turning mechanism*

The Crystal Palace was the brainchild of the Duke of Devonshire's head gardener and personal friend, Joseph Paxton (1801–1865), who got his idea whilst idly doodling on a blotting pad at a railway board meeting. Consisting basically of a huge prefabricated cast-iron frame and nearly 300,000 panes of glass, it was a logical development from Paxton's own conservatory at Chatsworth combined with a special greenhouse he had also built there to house an enormous and rare tropical water lily which he had successfully grown for the Duke in 1850.

The Crystal Palace was erected in Hyde Park, near the top of what is now Exhibition Road, South Kensington. The Exhibition itself lasted for just over five months, from May to October 1851, and when it was over discussion raged as to what to do with the building. Eventually it was taken down and re-erected, with some modifications, at Sydenham, where it stood until completely destroyed by fire during the night of 30 November 1936. Nothing can compensate for the loss of this supremely practical yet uniquely beautiful building, the prints and photographs that are all we have to remember it by today being but a poor substitute for the real thing.

The actual objects shown at the Great Exhibition – the first truly international event of its kind – ranged in size from the minute to huge pieces of heavy machinery. It is sometimes objected that the items such as furniture were mostly pure exhibition pieces, specially made for the occasion and not truly representative of the general trend of production and design at that time. Indeed, some Victorians themselves were aware of this: a contemporary comment on the furniture at the Crystal Palace reads: 'This magnificent display gave birth to one legitimate regret, that amidst all the ornamental works in furniture collected at the Exhibition, there were to be found so few specimens of ordinary furniture for general use.'[*] Yet as a modern writer has remarked, 'Exhibition furniture puts popular taste under a magnifying glass',[†] and certainly in its design and construction that same ordinary furniture quickly began to show the effects of the Exhibition, mainly and most obviously in the form of excessive over-decoration. The overloading with ornament and detail, whether on a carpet, a piece of silver or an object of furniture, was the inevitable result of a combination of different factors, including the abandonment of eighteenth-century traditions of individual craftsmanship, the introduction of new methods of mass-production, and new patronage by a new mercantile, rich and culturally uneducated middle class to whom art of any kind was simply another commodity to be bought and sold for cash.

'Ask a cabinet-maker', says Loudon, 'and he will tell you at once, that his

---

[*] Quoted by C. H. Gibbs-Smith in *The Great Exhibition of 1851*, an official publication of the Victoria and Albert Museum, p. 117. 1950.
[†] C. Handley-Read in *World Furniture*, ed. H. Hayward, p. 212. 1965.

customers prefer the ornamental chair, and care nothing about the unity, or the want of unity, of style. Their great object is to get a display of rich workmanship, at as cheap a rate as possible. Our readers, we are sure, will agree with us, that this taste on the part of the purchaser is of a vulgar and grovelling kind, and ought to be corrected.'

And so it was that the decline in popular taste, foreshadowed by George Smith's designs in the 1820s, reached its nadir in the 1850s, being highlighted by the Great Exhibition. Yet, paradoxically, the Exhibition itself was the starting point for a movement of reform which, for the rest of the nineteenth century and on into the twentieth, was to raise the levels of taste, design and craftsmanship for the benefit of those to whom such things were more important than money.

The principal name associated with the reform movement is of course that of William Morris (1834–96). Imbued from an early age with an enduring romantic, if idealised, vision of the Middle Ages, Morris was not only appalled but actually physically revolted by most of what he saw at the Great Exhibition. Mass-production, he felt, had destroyed the soul of the artist, whose self-

84 *Fireplace of the Great Parlour at Wightwick Manor, Staffordshire, 1887–1893. Morris decorations, wallpaper and upholstery*

respect could be regained only by a return to medieval methods of individual craftsmanship. (This chimed in also with his theories of social reform which led him in later life to spend an increasing amount of time and energy in preaching the doctrines of Socialism proper.) Accordingly in 1861 he founded, together with a circle of friends, the famous firm of Morris and Company which existed until the outbreak of the Second World War in 1939. The object of 'the Firm' (as they called it) was to design, make and sell good quality furniture, stained glass, embroidery, glass, metalwork, wallpaper, fabrics, tapestries and similar artifacts. To Morris, artist and craftsman were one and the same person, their functions indivisible. 'Art is the expression of man's pleasure in labour', he wrote, and again, 'Have nothing in your houses that you do not know to be useful and believe to be beautiful.'

Most of the Firm's early furniture was designed by Philip Webb (1831–1915) and Ford Madox Brown (1821–1893), mainly in the form of tables, chests-of-drawers and so on. It is plain, sturdy and (in the case of Webb) faintly Gothic. 'Our furniture should be good citizen's furniture, solid and well made in workmanship, and in design should have nothing about it that is not easily defensible, no monstrosities or extravagances, not even of beauty lest we weary of it', remarked Morris in an interesting lecture delivered in 1882, and he went on to say that 'except for very movable things like chairs, it should not be so very light as to be nearly imponderable; it should be made of timber rather than walking sticks.' Though usually it was left unpainted, Morris and his friends did revive the genuine practice of decorating furniture – especially pieces designed for their own homes – with painted scenes and decoration. Furthermore, their Gothic furniture gives a deliberate impression of being somewhat rough and ready, much more like the work of a medieval craftsman than anything so far seen in the revived Gothic style. Some of it was first displayed in public at the second largest international exhibition to be held in London, that of 1862. Morris himself never designed any furniture except some huge settles for a bachelor flat which he shared with the painter Burne-Jones in Red Lion Square. When the Firm was reorganised on a commercial basis in the early 1870s a craftsman named George Jack became the principal furniture designer.

Morris and his associates soon recognised that the Firm would have to supply its wares on two levels – expensive pieces specially commissioned by individual patrons, and commercial pieces in 'cottage' style for ordinary customers. Among the most popular items in the latter class were an adjustable-back upholstered easy chair and a plain rush-seated armchair (called 'the Sussex') based on traditional country models and produced in large numbers from 1865 onwards. By the 1870s the Sussex (or copies of it, many of which were made by other firms) was considered essential in every 'artistic' home. If it looks unremarkable to us today, we have to remember that at that time pieces of such extreme simplicity were normally tolerated only in the nursery or kitchen.

The Firm also supplied entire schemes of decoration for the houses or individual rooms of its patrons. A rare example of a completely preserved Morris and Company room is the former Green Dining Room in the Victoria and Albert Museum; though not a domestic interior it is sufficiently typical of one. It may seem dark and somewhat dingy to our taste, even allowing for the passage of time, but the individual style of the Firm is unmistakable in the moulded plaster decoration (designed by Philip Webb), being immediately recognisable as always by the use of naturalistic motifs deriving from plant and animal life, and reminiscent of the flower-strewn backgrounds of medieval tapestries so dear to the heart of Morris himself.

However, an even greater treasure house of the Morris movement is Wightwick Manor in Staffordshire. The house itself was built between 1887 and 1893 by Edward Ould, in an unusually convincing 'Tudor' style complete with gables, half-timbering and oriel windows on the exterior; the illusion is continued inside with period fireplaces, oak panelling, and a Great Parlour with an open timber roof and minstrels' gallery. Throughout the house the contents bear the stamp of Morris and his associates – his wallpapers (famous patterns with names such as the 'Leicester', 'Wild Lily', 'Daisy', 'Acanthus' and 'Willow-bough'), textiles including curtains, chair covers and tapestries, fine examples of carpets in the 'Hammersmith' and 'Lily' designs, and furniture such as examples of the Sussex chair. The house is also hung with paintings and drawings by Morris's friends including Rossetti, Burne-Jones, Madox Brown and Millais. It is the perfect antidote to a house such as Thoresby Hall, the perfect cure for artistic indigestion brought on by too much indulgence in High Victorian Gothic.

Not everyone who disliked the excesses of High Victorian art wished to go so far in the opposite direction as Morris, and middle-of-the-road designs for furniture were successfully produced by others working independently, notably the architects Bruce Talbert and T. E. Collcutt. Once again, too, the Orient raised its head in the shape of a vogue for Japanese-style furniture, mostly made of bamboo. This took place during the 1870s and '80s. Although the actual pieces owed more in their design to Europe than to Japan (where furniture is in any case comparatively scarce), the lightness of the bamboo was in welcome contrast to the heaviness of most commercial furniture of the time. Bamboo, Japanese screens and fans were moreover part of a process which gathered momentum and by the 1880s was identified with the aestheticism of Oscar Wilde and his set, unmercifully lampooned by W. S. Gilbert in *Patience* (1881).

William Morris stands as the link figure between the Gothic Revival on the one hand and the modernism of the Arts and Crafts movement on the other. This was really a blanket term for a variety of small groups of artists/craftsmen, all of whom shared a common veneration for the theories of Ruskin and Morris, together with a hatred of the prevailing low standards of commercial work-

85 *Ladder-back chair of ash with rush seat, designed and made by Ernest Gimson, about 1888. (V. and A. Museum)*

87   *The Red House, Bexleyheath, Kent. By Philip Webb for William Morris, 1859.*
A refreshingly new, practical and surprisingly modern approach to medievalism

the staircase being housed in a tower at the junction of the two wings. An important exterior feature is a well with a tall conical roof supported on stout timbers, standing in the courtyard formed by the angle of the wings. The Red House is not self-consciously Gothic, except in a few minor details, but it is more genuinely medieval in that it reflects in its deliberately irregular planning and outline the manor houses which Morris and his friends were now re-discovering with delight, especially in the Cotswold area. Eventually Morris himself was to settle his family in an ancient house of the same type, Kelmscott Manor in Oxfordshire, dating from about 1600.

The Red House is Webb's vision of a functional and practical medievalism, as opposed to the decorative approach of the Gothicists. Its liberating influence affected a number of architects whose clients wanted something different and 'modern', yet not so radical as the Red House (not that the house itself attracted much general attention at the time). Chief amongst these architects was Richard Norman Shaw (1831–1912), who successfully absorbed the main historical

88 *Cragside, Northumberland. By Richard Norman Shaw, 1870. Tudor elements predominate here, but the result is more reminiscent of a Bavarian hunting lodge*

styles and from them was able to produce a wide selection of houses ranging from the earliest examples of 'stockbrokers' Tudor' to 'Queen Anne'. His plans are irregular and always interesting, with part of the house very often being set at a slight angle to the rest. Cragside (Northumberland) is an example of baronial splendour less typical of Shaw, but Grims Dyke near Stanmore (Middlesex) is a fine example of Shaw at his quirky, pseudo-Tudor best.

Compared to the average country house in High Victorian Gothic, Shaw's houses look fresh and interesting, as indeed they are, for their conception is much more free and the ornament a good deal more restrained and authentic. But it is a mistake to regard Shaw as the first truly modern architect; that title might be given with greater justice to C. A. Voysey (1857–1941), though Voysey himself hated modernism and would certainly have disclaimed any such title.

Voysey's country houses, the ancestors of many others, are distinguished by their deceptively cottage-like appearance, all low silhouettes, gables, tall

89   *The Orchard, Chorleywood, Hertfordshire. By C. F. A. Voysey, 1900. Not at first sight outstanding, simply because so many apparently similar houses have been built since then*

chimneys and mullioned casement windows. Inside, the same impression is fostered by the use of such features as low beamed ceilings, tiled fireplaces, inglenooks (also used by Shaw) and cottage-style doors with latches. There is much use of white paint both within and without. This is the country cottage as seen through the rose-tinted spectacles of the well-to-do middle class country dweller. A good example is 'The Orchard', a private house at Chorleywood (Hertfordshire), which Voysey built for himself in 1900. Another is 'Broadleys' (1898), on Lake Windermere.

Voysey's style is echoed – though often on a much more imposing style – by E. W. Lutyens (1869–1944). The two main influences on Lutyens' architecture may be said to have been the Tudor manor house and the late seventeenth-, early eighteenth-century so-called Queen Anne style. Lutyens' great *forte* was the ability to understand and use the elements of both styles so successfully that his houses are not so much imitations as re-creations. The unwary visitor could be forgiven for supposing that Great Maytham Hall, near Rolveden in Kent, was

90   *Entrance hall of The Orchard. Note the long hinges and small tulip-shaped latch on the right-hand door; these contain the seeds of Art Nouveau*

built about 1700 instead of 1910, or that Munstead Wood, near Godalming in Surrey, was Tudor and not late Victorian (1896). The illusion is not confined only to exteriors, for while not in any way compromising on the demands for late nineteenth- and twentieth-century comforts, Lutyens fills his interiors with appropriate fittings and decoration such as oak beams, panelling, rich plaster-work, and staircase balustrades of turned wood or ironwork.

To Lutyens belongs the distinction of having built what must almost certainly be the last of the great English country houses, in every sense of the word. Castle Drogo (Devonshire) was designed and built in 1910–30 for a rich business man, Julius Drewe. Massively constructed of granite, it is basically a tall, long and narrow building angled at the centre, the exterior reminding one in parts of a medieval castle complete with battlements and working portcullis, in others of the late Tudor prodigy houses, especially Hardwick Hall. This latter likeness is conveyed most forcibly by a series of angled bays with oriel windows on each of the three floors. The true castle atmosphere is reinforced

91   *Tigbourne Court, Witley, Surrey. By E. W. Lutyens, 1899–1901. Tudor and seventeenth-century elements mingled to produce a pleasing fantasy*

92   *Castle Drogo, Devonshire. By E. W. Lutyens, 1910–1930. Back to where it all began – the medieval castle*

inside by much use of bare unplastered granite and by unpainted woodwork. The romanticism of castle architecture had a special appeal for Lutyens, who successfully restored as a dwelling a small semi-ruined fortress on Holy Island, off the coast of Northumberland.

The connection between Hardwick and Castle Drogo is not merely superficial, it is right and fitting, for the one stands almost at the beginning of that long line of country houses whose purpose – whatever their style – was primarily to advertise the wealth and social status of the owner, whilst the other surely concludes the same line.

CHAPTER EIGHT

The Garden Setting

THE GARDEN is as much a part of the English country house as are its furniture and fittings, and is a work of art in its own right, though of comparatively recent development. Without doubt the Roman villas had gardens, but we know very little about them and all traces of them were swept away during the Dark Ages. In the troubled centuries that followed the withdrawal of the Roman army from our shores only the monasteries maintained gardens, and these were devoted mainly to the growing of vegetables and the cultivation of herbs for medicinal and culinary purposes. As times became safer it does seem as though small formal flower gardens grew up within the walls of great castles. But not many castles would have had space for such a luxury, and our ideas of what such medieval gardens may have looked like (enclosed within little walls and trellises, with fountains, basins, statuary and arbours) are culled entirely from Continental sources, for no English illustrations of them exist.

Not until the Tudor period do we get any clear picture of the development of our gardens. We then find that the influence of the Renaissance made itself felt in this as in other spheres. The gardens of Renaissance Italy were planned on highly formal lines, their paths and terraces forming geometric patterns punctuated at carefully measured intervals by fountains and statuary. This was the style followed for the first time in France by Francis I at his new palace of Fontainebleu, and thence copied by Henry VIII for *his* new palace of Nonsuch; thus, not for the first time, an important element of Renaissance art reached us at second hand via France.

Nowadays the best-known feature of the Tudor garden is surely the knot, in fashion by the time of Elizabeth I. On raised square or rectangular beds were formed patterns – increasingly complex as time went on – made from geometrical lines of clipped herbs or shrubs such as thrift or dwarf box, with the spaces between them filled in with gravel, sand, minerals, shrubs or flowers. Flowers, in fact, though loved, were not so carefully tended and cultivated as they are today, and indeed seem to have been looked on mainly as decorative in-filling for the knots. (It is possible that the phrase 'nuts in May', from the well-known nursery rhyme, in fact refers to knots of may, clusters of spring flowers traditionally gathered in the fields on May Day.) Knot gardens did not please everybody. In a little essay entitled *Of Gardens* (1625) Francis Bacon wrote scathingly: 'As for the making of knots or figures, with divers coloured earths ... they be but toys: you may see as good sights, many times, in tarts' (referring presumably to the criss-cross, lattice-like pastry decorations still to be seen today on, for example, treacle tarts).

No original Tudor gardens survive today, and we can only reconstruct them, as for example in the sunken garden at Hampton Court or at New Place, Stratford-upon-Avon. Their basic plan was one of small, self-sufficient enclosures, and this still held good in 1625 when Bacon wrote: 'The garden is best to be square, encompassed on all the four sides with a stately arched hedge' (*Of Gardens*). These enclosures were enlivened with statues, of lead as well as stone, and relieved by expanses of grass on which games such as bowls and tennis were played. 'Nothing is more pleasant to the eye than green grass kept finely shorn', remarks Bacon, shearing being done by scythe until the invention of the lawn mower in 1831. A feature of most large gardens was a mount, an artificial mound crowned with a seat, arbour or small garden house from which one could have a bird's-eye view of the whole garden, reached by steps or a path that spiralled up the sides of the mount: one may be found in the reconstructed Dutch Garden at Kew and at Packwood House in Warwickshire.

Jacobean gardens differed little in their general planning and appearance from Tudor ones, so far as can be judged from old plans, prints and descriptions, except that the larger of them became even more formal and stately. But as with the other arts, a great change took place at the Restoration. English post-1660 garden design owes nothing to the Tudors and nothing directly to Italy. Instead the two new sources of influence were France and Holland.

In France the formal garden, originally Italian-influenced as we have seen, assumed in the mid-seventeenth century a completely individual character of its own at the hands of the brilliant garden planner André Le Nôtre. To Le Nôtre the garden was no longer a place in which to find secluded peace but a stage setting, a backcloth against which the puppet-like figures of court society could act out their lives in public; for this reason, he felt, it should be possible to appreciate the main details and outlines of the garden at a single glance. A restricted view was intolerable; wide walks and great, sweeping panoramic views were the order of the day, as can be seen on visiting Le Nôtre's masterpiece, the gardens of Versailles. The plan of this huge and stupendous setting for the palace of Louis XIV shows immediately how the entire grounds were designed on a series of axes radiating from the palace itself, emphasising the supremacy of Louis himself as the Sun King from whom all things stemmed, and the fact that it is Man and not Nature who rules in this garden. The overall design, too, is seen to have a grid-like, geometrical rigidity that characterises not only the paths and avenues but also the formal ponds and canals that now

93   *Hampton Court. In the Sunken Garden a good attempt has been made to recreate the spirit, if not the letter, of a Tudor garden*

have an increasingly important part to play. Moreover, enormous jets of water issuing from dozens of carefully-sculpted fountains were an integral part of the Le Nôtre garden, forming punctuation points at measured intervals. (Their impact, however, was seldom total, for both at Versailles and elsewhere there seems always to have been difficulty in getting enough pressure to raise the water sufficiently high.)

The development of the Le Nôtre French-style garden in this country was due mainly to George London (d. 1714) and his partner Henry Wise (1653–1738), who together kept a nursery garden at Brompton, on the site of the present museums in South Kensington. From here they supplied most of the great gardens in the land with plants, shrubs and even semi-grown trees. Whilst Wise looked after the nursery, London rode round the country, averaging it is said between 50 and 60 miles per day, executing commissions in garden design. He had twice visited France and had met Le Nôtre, so was well fitted to introduce French ideas and practices. Above all he prompted the idea of the parterre as a replacement for the knot. In the parterre the principle of patterning remains, but the patterns are of a much more flowing type; indeed, parterres were called 'broderies' and pattern books were published in which the designs could be used either for garden parterres or for actual embroidery. Furthermore, whereas each knot garden was an individual self-contained enclosure, each parterre was designed to be seen in relation to a much wider overall scheme. One of the finest parterres ever to be made in this country was constructed by Wise and London at Chatsworth; here the designs (the largest measuring 473 by 227 feet) were formed from turf, soil, gravel, sand and minerals. (On other occasions the dust of coal and bricks was also used.) A reconstructed parterre may be seen at Blenheim; formed early during the present century, it recalls the original one designed by Wise but swept away during the landscaping craze of the eighteenth century when formal lines in a garden became anathema. This craze, indeed, is the reason why no original parterres still exist, as will be shown later in this chapter.

Flowers normally had no part in the formality of a parterre, for they refused to keep to rules and obscured the clear outlines of the designs. Instead they were kept at a distance in formal beds called compartments, or massed in walled enclosures such as kitchen gardens. Pepys records an interesting conversation that he held in 1666 with Hugh May, the architect, in which, during a general discussion on gardening, they agreed that 'flowers . . . are best seen in a little plot by themselves: besides, their borders spoil the walks of another garden.' During the course of the same conversation they also agreed that 'we have the best walks of gravel in the world, France having none, nor Italy; and the green of our bowling alleys is better than any they have.'

It is interesting to note that the French invented the word *boulingrin* to denote an area of turf sunk somewhat below ground level, with sloping edges. One does not at first recognise in this the English 'bowling green' which is in fact the source of the French term, though the actual game of bowls as played in this country has remained a mystery to the French.

Beyond the parterres blocks of woodland were introduced as contrast. The word blocks is used here purposely, for in the engravings of the period (for example, in *Vitruvius Britannicus*) such woodland has a solid appearance, as though it were literally carved from a solid block of wood. It is divided up geometrically by alleyways and glades, which open out every so often into spaces containing points of punctuation such as obelisks, statues or fountains. These wooded areas were known as 'boskets', from the French *bosquet* meaning a grove or thicket. There was a large bosket at Hampton Court of which only the core now remains; this is the famous Maze, originally laid out by Wise in about 1690 and described then as 'a figure hedge work of large evergreen plants' (in fact yew, though now mainly replaced by privet). Wise probably used the foundations of an old Tudor maze. (Properly speaking, a maze – the origins are lost in the mists of antiquity – is laid out plan-like on the ground; when it becomes three-dimensional as at Hampton Court it is then a labyrinth.)

It was Wise who carried out most of the garden planning at Hampton Court, though some advice was taken from Daniel Marot (see p. 43). Wise's main achievement was to lay out the Great Fountain Court, on the main garden front of the palace, with 13 fountains set in one enormous parterre. The plan was the

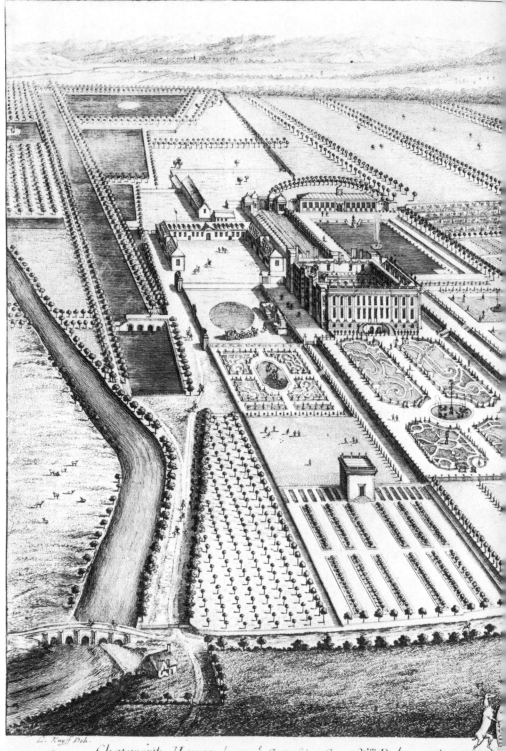

L. Knyff Del.

Chatsworth House being ij Seat of his Grace Wᵐ Duke and
of her Maᵗⁱᵉˢ housˢhold, Chief Iustice in Eyre of all her Maᵗⁱᵉˢ Forrests Chaces Parks

CAVEN

Earl of Devonshire, Marquis of Hartington, Baron of Hardwick, L.d Steward
&c. Trent. North and K.t of the Most Noble Order of the Garter —
Printed & Sold by I. Smith at ÿ Sign of Exeter Change in ÿ Strand.

94 *The gardens of Chatsworth, as created by Henry Wise and George London à la*
Versailles. *From* Nouveau Théâtre de la Grande Bretagne, *engraved by J. Kip from*
a drawing by L. Knyff, 1724

very French one of a *patte d'oie* or goose foot, a semicircle with paths and/or canals radiating from it. Most of the fountains have now vanished and the lines of the main design are obscured by tree growth, but in theory a satisfactory restoration of the area would be entirely feasible.

Wise's parterre at Blenheim has already been briefly mentioned. Beyond it he laid out the 'Great Woodwork', a formal wilderness some 500 by 600 yards in extent, divided up into symmetrical boskets. A remarkable feature of the garden as a whole – and a delicate compliment to the Duke of Marlborough – was its inclusion within an enormous star-shaped bastion wall on the model of Continental fortifications of the period. Of this grand design nothing now remains except the walled kitchen garden.

The gardens of seventeenth-century Holland could not, of course, remain entirely uninfluenced by those of France, but certain native characteristics were imposed upon the French style. Dutch gardens were on the whole cosier, far more inward-looking and sectional, even if the larger examples did boast French items such as parterres and boskets. The flat landscapes and grid-like canal patterns of Holland did not allow for grand vistas, cascades and fountains, so these were compensated for by greater attention to detail – Versailles in miniature, so to speak.

It was this type of garden for which William and Mary brought considerable enthusiasm on their accession in 1688. William in particular is said to have been especially garden-conscious, and to have taken great interest in the provision of ornamental evergreen shrubs. Many owners of the smaller English country houses now found the Dutch-style garden more suited to their means than the grandiose French conception, and numerous examples may be seen in the delightful series of plates showing various country seats engraved about 1700 by Badeslade, Kip and others. A reasonably successful modern reconstruction of a Dutch garden has been attempted behind the so-called Dutch House in Kew Gardens, but the best-preserved original garden of this type (specifically a water-garden) is the recently-restored one at Westbury Court in Gloucestershire. The gardens of Ham House, much admired in their day, will when restored take on once again their original Dutch character.

The inward-looking nature of the Dutch garden was also expressed in the mania for topiary work. Topiary was not new, and indeed had been very popular also in Tudor and Jacobean times, though not universally so: Bacon writes scornfully of 'images cut out in juniper or other garden stuff: they be for children'. There is an impressive topiary garden at Packwood, Warwickshire, dating from about 1650, in which the arrangement of the bushes is said to represent the scene of the Sermon on the Mount. However, for extensive topiary conceived under the Dutch influence one should go to Levens Hall near Kendal; here the garden dates from about 1700 and was laid out by a Monsieur Beaumont who, though said to have been a pupil of Le Nôtre, nevertheless followed Dutch rather than French ideals at Levens.

95 *Kew, the Dutch House. The re-created Dutch garden, neatly complementing the riverside façade*

Care is necessary in dating topiary work. Some is genuinely old, as at Pack-wood, Levens, and Chastleton (said to date, like that at Levens, from about 1700). But topiary in general fits in so well with ancient buildings that at Compton Wynyates, for example, it comes as something of a shock to learn that the topiary garden there dates only from 1895.

Sooner or later there was bound to be a reaction against the formal French and Dutch gardens, with their geometrical layout, their parterres, fountains, topiary and so on. A pioneer in promoting a new sense of freedom, however tentative, was Charles Bridgeman, who had been Wise's apprentice at the Brompton Nurseries and succeeded him as royal gardener, though both died in 1738. One of Bridgeman's great gardens was at Stowe, Buckinghamshire, and the plan of the grounds (published after his death by his widow) shows that, though the main paths and avenues continue to follow lines of geometrical severity, minor paths begin to meander with new diversity. A contemporary of Bridgeman, Stephen Switzer, also produced plans, and gardens based on them, on notably less severe lines.

But such hesitant steps towards a new informality in garden design were quite overshadowed by the work of the Palladian school, in particular William Kent, whom Walpole calls 'the father of modern gardening', declaring in a famous phrase that Kent 'leaped the fence and saw that all Nature is a garden' –

in other words, that he finally abolished the divisions between what lay inside a garden and what outside, what was natural and what artificial. But it must be clearly recognised that the spirit of informality engendered by this new philosophy had nothing haphazard about it. Inspired as always by Italian classicism, what Kent and his contemporaries set out to do was to create in terms of real landscape the painted landscapes of the school of Claude Lorraine, the seventeenth-century French-born painter who lived and worked in Italy. The landscapes of Claude show us a timeless classical Arcadia, carefully composed on canvas in the studio and never painted in the open air from nature (though sketches, made on the spot, were used in assembling the final harmonious composition). The figures in them appear as though against a theatrical backdrop, and any story they may tell, be it Biblical or mythological, is of secondary importance. In a Claude painting, the landscape is all.

A prime mover in the new approach to garden design was the poet Alexander Pope, who at his villa in Twickenham had in 1718 begun just such a garden, miniature in size but far-reaching in its effect upon men such as Kent and Lord Burlington; the shaping of it took Pope some 25 years. Its effect on Kent was first seen at Chiswick, where the famous Villa was set in the first large garden in this country to be designed throughout on the principle of what might be called planned informality, where the hand of Nature was not forced so much as carefully guided by Man. In breaking down barriers between the natural and the artificial Kent was the first to understand the full possibilities of the ha-ha or sunken ditch, which avoids the use of a fence whilst keeping animals away from the immediate vicinity of a house. Despite its name, the element of humour does not enter into the ha-ha. The first English reference to it is apparently in a 1712 translation of a French work on formal gardens, in which we are told that the ha-ha 'surprises the eye on coming near it and makes one cry Ah! Ah! from whence it takes its name'.

The plan of Chiswick (now being gradually restored) was based on main axes radiating from the house, between which were wooded areas broken up by meandering paths. A feature of the Kentian garden, as of painted landscapes of the Claude school, was the number of small temple buildings, statues, obelisks and so on that punctuated the landscape and acted as eye-catchers and focal points. At Chiswick the obelisk and the temple in the lake still remain, as do the man-made terraces of what was then the Orange Garden. Here, it is said, Kent sat throughout the whole of a warm summer night in a kind of trance, bemused by the beauty of the setting which he himself had created. Orange trees in tubs adorned the terraces, brought out when the weather became sufficiently warm, and rushed back again into the shelter of the Orangery at the first hint of autumn frosts.

Much architectural skill went into the designing of the many ornamental features – the temples, urns and so on – that now became such an important part of the classically-inspired landscape. At Chiswick Lord Burlington designed several of the buildings himself. At Stowe Kent provided the strange Temple of British Worthies, a gallery of niches containing busts of the famous. At Rousham in Oxfordshire he provided a graceful arcade; indeed Rousham is probably both the best and the best-preserved of Kent's work in garden design, where one can still see the principles advocated by Pope brought to their final perfection. Those principles Pope had neatly summarised in the fourth of his *Moral Essays*, first published in 1731 and addressed to Lord Burlington, of which the following short extract must serve as an example:

> To build, to plant, whatever you intend,
> To rear the column, or the arch to bend,
> To swell the terrace, or to sink the grot,
> In all, let nature never be forgot . . .

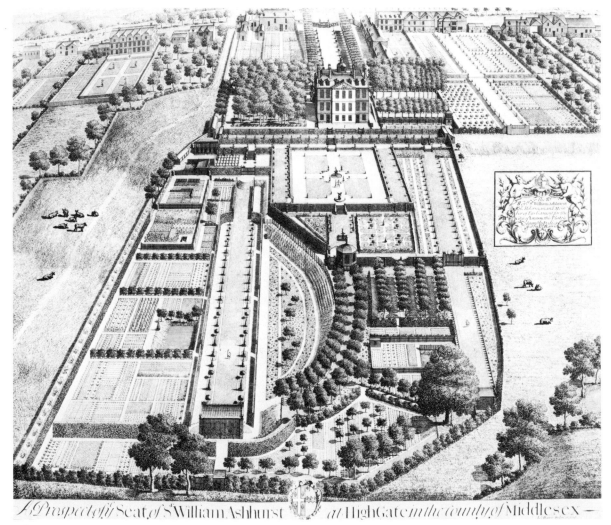

96 *An example of the smaller, inward looking Dutch-style garden. By J. Harris in* Nouveau Théâtre de la Grande Bretagne, *1724*

97 *Print showing part of the gardens at Chiswick House, as laid out by Kent. These alleys may still be traced and the Rustic House (at the end of the right-hand alley) still survives.*

Consult the genius of the place in all,
That tells the waters or to rise, or fall. . . .
Now breaks, or now directs, the intending lines,
Paints as you plant, and as you work, designs.*

One of the most remarkable gardens to reveal the new feeling for landscaping is Stourhead, remarkable because, firstly, it still exists unaltered except for natural growth and new plantings, and secondly, because it was the work of an amateur who apparently had no professional help of any kind. The banker Henry Hoare inherited his family estate in 1741 (his father had engaged Colen Campbell to design the house, see p. 62), and began work on the garden at once, completing it in about 1772. In it he not only followed the still basically formal naturalism of Kent, but actually anticipated the completely informal naturalism of Capability Brown. The garden is planted round the banks of a large, irregularly-shaped lake (such lakes or ponds being an important feature of the style in general). Its ornamental details, cunningly inserted into the landscape,

*Alexander Pope was the most brilliant literary star of the Palladian circle and consistently supported Palladian theories and personalities in his own work.

are typical of their kind; they include the Sun Temple (copied from an original at Baalbec), the temple-like Pantheon, a large medieval stone cross (in fact the original central cross erected in Bristol in 1373), a Rustic Cottage and a Grotto. This last was common to almost all gardens of the period, even Pope's; the inner walls were usually set with pebbles, shells or minerals. The Stourhead Grotto is an especially large and fine example, and contains large white-painted figures of the River God and the Nymph of the Grot. Connoisseurs of eighteenth-century epitaphs as well as those of gardens may be interested to read the following lines which are inscribed on Henry Hoare's tomb in the parish church at Stourhead:

> Ye who have view'd in Pleasure's choicest Hour
> The Earth embellished on these Banks of Stour,
> With grateful Reverence to this Marble lean
> Rais'd to the Friendly Founder of the Scene.
> Here, with pure love of smiling Nature warm'd,
> This far-fam'd Demi-Paradise he form'd:
> And, happier still, here learn'd from Heaven to find
> A sweeter Eden in a Bounteous Mind.
> Thankful these fair & flowery paths he trod,
> And priz'd them only as they lead to God.

It is safe to say that the best-known name of all English garden designers is that of Lancelot Brown (1715–83), whose nickname 'Capability' came from his habit of referring to the 'capabilities' of any site to which he was called with a view to its alteration. In 1740 Brown, then an ambitious young man already well grounded in the science and art of gardening, entered the service of Lord Cobham at Stowe. Here he came inevitably under the influence of Kent who was creating the grounds at the time, and from a close study of Kent's aims and methods formulated his own theories of landscape gardening, theories which were literally to change entirely the garden face of England. Brown was called in his time to most of the great estates in the land, as well as to many lesser ones; there is hardly a garden of any size or note in the country where his hand is not alleged to have appeared, in legend if not in fact, and much of his planning still remains unchanged.

The basic ingredients of Brown's style are generous plantations, a serpentine river or lake, and trees (usually oak or chestnut) grouped in clumps on lawns around the house (though Kent was the first to introduce such clumps). His guiding principle was that Nature abhors a straight line, and even where ground was flat he caused it to undulate in a faithful imitation of naturalism. This theory inevitably led to the final destruction of the great formal gardens, with their parterres, fountain courts and boskets. 'So closely did he copy nature', remarked Horace Walpole, 'that his works will be mistaken for it.' Yet it is salutary to recall that most of Brown's work was an act of faith, for of necessity

98   *A corner of Stourhead, Wiltshire, showing the Pantheon and the Rustic Cottage.*

many years elapsed before his artificial landscaping took on the entirely natural appearance that he envisaged from the outset.

In 1751 he moved to London where he also took up architecture, almost as a sideline, though designing several Palladian-style houses of which Croome Court (Worcestershire) is the most important. Later, however, this part of his practice devolved upon his partner and son-in-law Henry Holland, a distinguished architect in his own right (see p. 154). In 1764 Brown became the Royal Surveyor of the Gardens at Hampton Court, where he supervised the planting of the still-extant Great Vine. To his credit it is said that he declined George III's invitation to landscape the palace gardens; perhaps he had noted the alarm that was being expressed in some quarters at what was felt to be his destructive approach to gardening. 'If this mania be not checked, there will not remain three trees standing in a line throughout the kingdom', growled Sir William Chambers, and certainly one cannot help wishing today that just one large formal garden could have been spared Brown's onslaughts.

One of the chief criticisms levelled at Brown by his contemporaries was that he allowed absolute naturalism – mostly in the form of grass – to come right up to the very walls of a house without insulation from Nature. The only man to continue most of his principles and to attain equal fame with him differed from him in restoring a certain amount of insulation in the form of paths, terraces, arbours, formal beds and the like. This was Humphry Repton (1752–1818), a failed business man from Norwich who turned his hand to landscape gardening without any training but with instant success. For his clients Repton (who, like Brown, also dabbled in architecture) prepared his famous Red Books, notebooks showing the proposed improvements to their estates by means of ingenious 'before-and-after' effects produced by flaps and moveable segments. Though each estate got a hand-produced Red Book to itself, some of the designs were later reproduced in book form in 1803 and 1816.

Repton's fame secured him honourable contemporary mention in Jane Austen's *Mansfield Park* (1814). In chapter six Mr Rushworth complains that his estate, Sotherton Court, 'wants improvement', and is urged by Miss Bertram and Mrs Norris to employ Mr Repton.

> 'That is what I was thinking of', remarks Mr Rushworth. 'As he has done so well by Smith [the friend whose 'improvements' have made him so dissatisfied with his own Sotherton] I think I had better have him at once. His terms are five guineas a day. . . . Smith's place is the admiration of all the country; and it was a mere nothing before Repton took it in hand. I think I shall have Repton.'

It should be noted that although Repton's grander designs are at first sight textbook Capability Brown he nonetheless had a somewhat different approach to landscaping than his predecessor. In Brown's schemes the house stands out proudly in its setting like a jewel in a ring or an island in an ocean. In those of Repton it merges into the landscape in the 'picturesque' manner favoured by Repton himself and by John Nash, who for a time was Repton's partner (see p. 137).

Repton's theories, modified and updated, were communicated to a wider gardening public in the writings of J. C. Loudon (see p. 160), who added gardening to the wide range of subjects on which – with some justification – he set himself up as an expert. In 1822 he produced *An Encyclopaedia of Gardening* and in 1838 *The Suburban Gardener and Villa Companion*. These works helped to bring the vistas of Repton within the confines of the small garden. The mixture of the formal and informal remained exactly the same, though as usual the Victorians took something from almost every century and style previous to their own. At Culzean Castle (see p. 131) there survives a small garden of the 1840s containing bamboos, pampas grass, a rockery, trees, shrubberies and a rustic summer house. Certain items and plants are permanently associated with the Victorian garden, such as wellingtonias, acacias, monkey puzzles, privet, cast-iron 'rustic' garden furniture, rhododendrons and laurels. (Laurel, it was believed, gave back unusually large amounts of oxygen into the atmosphere, and was therefore beneficial to health.) Paths were narrow, gravelled and winding. The overriding impression communicated by most Victorian gardens was one of extreme dullness and lack of any kind of horticultural inspiration. The discovery and provision of many new shrubs and plants during the period did

99 a & b   *Humphry Repton's proposed 'improvements' for West Wycombe Park,*
Buckinghamshire, in the form of before-and-after views (obtained by a moveable segment)

little to alter the situation, for there was hardly any appreciation of how to make the best of such riches except in the regimented form known as 'carpet-bedding'. The only Victorian gardens to differ from this type of thing were those of certain large houses in which a return was made to the extreme and rather arid formality of the Italian Renaissance style; this was promoted especially by the architect Sir Charles Barry (for example, at Shrubland Park, Suffolk, and at Harewood House).

The general Victorian attitude towards the garden persisted until the late nineteenth century, specifically until 1883. In that year a gardening expert named William Robinson (1839–1935) produced a book, *The English Flower Garden*, in which he finally demolished the concept of the formal garden, replacing it with that of the cottage garden in which plants were allowed to grow and flourish naturally without regimentation. (He had already anticipated this approach in an earlier book, *The Wild Garden*, 1870.) In 1884 he bought Gravetye Manor in Sussex, where he spent the rest of his long life in putting his gardening principles into practice; after suffering some neglect the garden has now been restored to something like Robinson's original conception.

Robinson's theories were improved, expanded and perfected by the fruitful collaboration of the architect Edwin Lutyens and Miss Gertrude Jekyll (1843–1932), who took to garden design when bad eyesight forced her to abandon the arts of painting and embroidery. Munstead Wood (1896, Surrey), Miss Jekyll's own house, was the first of many successful joint ventures in which house and garden complemented each other and were in fact designed from the outset as an entity. The 'cottage garden style' promoted by this partnership remains the inspiration behind very many gardens, both large and small, to be found throughout the country today.

Some Houses for Visiting in England

The following list (which is arranged in alphabetical order of counties) gives only those houses which, for one reason or another, the visitor should make special efforts to see. It should be supplemented by the publication *Historic houses, castles & gardens in Great Britain and Ireland*, issued annually by ABC Historic Publications and available at most larger bookshops. In fact, no visitor should be without this invaluable work, which lists all houses and similar properties open to the public, together with their precise locations, opening hours, facilities and other essential information.

Avon (formerly Bath/Bristol area)

Dodington House, near Chipping Sodbury. By James Wyatt. A fine classical mansion, and his last work, begun 1798. (See p. 135)

Buckinghamshire

Claydon House, near Winslow. Eighteenth century. Remaining wing of a much larger house. Notable for its unique Chinoiserie carvings. (See p. 98)

Cheshire

Little Moreton Hall, Congleton. 1559–1589. Well-known example of decorative half-timbering. (See p. 14)

Cornwall

Antony House, Torpoint. 1711–1721. One of the finest unspoilt houses of its period in the West Country.

Cotehele House, Calstock. 1485–1539. Fine medieval house, largely unaltered.

Cumbria

Levens Hall, near Kendal. Typical small Northern fortress-house transformed into an Elizabethan mansion about 1580. Noted for its seventeenth-century topiary garden. (See p. 194)

Derbyshire

Haddon Hall, near Bakewell. Medieval fortified house with later enlargements. (See p. 15)

Hardwick Hall, near Chesterfield. 1591–1597. One of the finest of the prodigy houses. (See p. 24)

Kedleston Hall, Derby. 1757–1765. Completed by Robert Adam in his noblest manner. (See p. 107)

Sudbury Hall, near Uttoxeter. Seventeenth century. Arguably the finest plasterwork of any house of its period in the country. (See p. 46)

Devonshire

Castle Drogo, near Chagford. By Sir Edwin Lutyens, 1910–1930. A modern prodigy house, the last of its kind. (See p. 185)

Saltram House, Plymouth. Sixteenth to eighteenth century. Incorporating two rooms decorated by Robert Adam. (See p. 98)

Dorset

Athelhampton. A very fine medieval house.

Essex

Audley End, Saffron Walden. Begun 1603. A prodigy house, now greatly reduced in size but still gigantic. (See p. 24)

Greater Manchester

Heaton Hall, Prestwich. By James Wyatt, 1772. Contains one of the few surviving Etruscan rooms of the period. (See p. 113)

Hampshire

The Vyne, Basingstoke. Sixteenth century with eighteenth-century additions and 1654 portico. (See p. 61)

Hertfordshire

Ashridge, Berkhamsted. By James Wyatt, begun 1808. Large Gothic mansion. (See p. 0)

Hatfield House, Hatfield. Built for Robert Cecil between 1607 and 1611. One of the most impressive of the prodigy houses. (See p. 24)

Kent

Great Maytham Hall, Rolveden. A Lutyens re-creation in 'Queen Anne' style, 1910. (See p. 184)

Ightham Mote, Ivy Hatch. A medieval manor house that has retained its original moat.

Knole, Sevenoaks, Dating from 1456, with seventeenth-century interiors. Noted for its unique collection of seventeenth- and eighteenth-century furniture. (See p. 32)

Penshurst Place, Tonbridge. Dating from 1340. The Great Hall is especially fine. (See p. 15)

Leicestershire

Belgrave Hall, Leicester. 1709–1713. An interesting example of the smaller, individual house of its period.

Belvoir Castle, near Grantham. Remodelled by Wyatt in 1816 into a mock medieval castle. (See p. 135)

Lincolnshire

Belton House, Grantham. 1685. A good example of the Pratt-influenced house, containing authentic carving by Grinling Gibbons. (See p. 46)

London

Chiswick House. By Lord Burlington, 1725. Decorations by William Kent. A visit to Chiswick is basic to a proper understanding of Palladianism. (See p. 64)

Fenton House, Hampstead. 1693. A charming house of its period, also containing a
  collection of keyboard musical instruments and another of porcelain.
Ham House, near Richmond. A Jacobean mansion altered during the post-Restoration
  period. Well documented and still containing most of the original furniture and
  fittings. (See p. 40)
Marble Hill House, Twickenham. A good example of a smallish Palladian villa.
Osterley Park House, near Hounslow. A Tudor mansion altered and furnished by
  Robert Adam and containing some of his finest inspirations. (See p. 106)
Syon House, Brentford. A medieval convent also altered inside by Adam. (See p. 106)

Norfolk

Holkham Hall, Wells. Designed in 1734 by William Kent in consultation with Lord
  Burlington and the owner, Lord Leicester. Also contains furniture and decoration by
  Kent. (See p. 66)
Houghton Hall, King's Lynn. By Colen Campbell for Sir Robert Walpole. Interiors by
  Kent. (See p. 62)

Northamptonshire

Burghley House, near Stamford. A prodigy house, also containing some of Antonio
  Verrio's finest decorative painting. (See p. 49)
Lamport Hall, near Northampton. An interesting seventeenth- to eighteenth-century
  house, part of it by John Webb, containing some good plasterwork.

Northumberland

Lindisfarne Castle, Holy Island. About 1550. Cleverly converted soon after 1900 by
Lutyens. (See p. 187)
Seaton Delaval Hall, Whitley Bay. By Vanbrugh, 1718–1728. Huge, rambling mansion
  in his most theatrical manner, though now (through fire, etc.) a mere shadow of its
  former self.

Nottinghamshire

Thoresby Hall, Ollerton. By Anthony Salvin, 1864. Fine example of Jacobethan
  baronial. (See p. 161)
Wollaton Hall, Nottingham. A great and unusually-planned prodigy house, not happy
  in its present-day rôle as a natural history museum. (See p. 26)

Oxfordshire

Blenheim Palace. Vanbrugh's masterpiece, completed by Hawksmoor. Comment
  would be superfluous. (See p. 58)
Chastleton House, near Moreton-in-Marsh. 1603. A little-known but fascinating
  Jacobean mansion containing many unsuspected delights.
Mapledurham House, near Reading. Late sixteenth century. Remarkable sequence of
  original moulded plaster ceilings.

Shropshire

Benthall Hall, Much Wenlock. Sixteenth-century stone-built manor house.
Mawley Hall, Cleobury Mortimer. Early eighteenth century. Fine plasterwork and
  woodwork of its period.

Somerset

Montacute House, Yeovil. Begun 1588. Impressive Elizabethan mansion.

Tintinhull House, Yeovil. Small seventeenth-century manor house with eighteenth-century façade grafted on.

Suffolk

Heveningham Hall, near Halesworth. By Sir Robert Taylor, 1779. Interior 1781–84 by James Wyatt in his best manner; includes another Etruscan room.

Surrey

Clandon Park, near Guildford. By Giacomo Leoni, 1731–1735. Its cube-like form is a useful corrective to the idea that all Palladian houses are basically alike from outside.

Warwickshire

Compton Wynyates, Tysoe. 1480–1520. Perfect example of the later fortified manor house. (See p. 12)

Packwood House, Hockley Heath. Early sixteenth-century with additions between 1660 and 1670. Has undergone some restoration, but still charming.

West Midlands

Aston Hall, Birmingham. 1618–35. One of the last of the prodigy houses, but in no way inferior to any other. (See p. 30)

Wightwick Manor, Wolverhampton, 1887–1893. A text-book interior of furnishing and decoration by William Morris and his associates. (See p. 178)

West Sussex

Petworth House, Petworth. Rebuilt 1688–1696. Contains some of Grinling Gibbons's finest work (to say nothing of Turner's paintings).

Uppark, near Petersfield. 1690. Furnished between 1750 and 1770, and mainly un-altered since then.

Wiltshire

Littlecote, near Hungerford. About 1490–1520. An early Tudor manor house of great charm and historic interest.

Stourhead, Stourton, near Mere. By Colen Campbell, 1722. A good example of the smaller Palladian house, though not completed to Campbell's plan until the nineteenth century. The grounds constitute one of the earliest and most famous essays in landscape gardening in the country. (See pp. 198–9)

Wilton House, near Salisbury. In part by Inigo Jones, about 1650. The beauty and importance of the Double Cube Room cannot be too often stressed. (See pp. 35–6)

Yorkshire

Castle Howard. By Vanbrugh, 1699–1726. Vanbrugh's first great house, but in no way a tentative attempt. (See p. 60)

Newby Hall, Ripon. A seventeenth-century house enlarged by Robert Adam. The Sculpture Gallery was specially designed to house the owner's collection of classical statues, and as such typifies the contemporary interest in classicism in general.

Nostell Priory, Wakefield. By James Paine, 1733, with additions by Adam, 1766. Interior mainly by Adam and containing some famous items of genuine Chippendale furniture. (See p. 88)

Temple Newsam, near Leeds. Tudor house with eighteenth-century additions. Now a museum housing notable pieces of furniture including the Chippendale library table from Harewood House. (See p. 92)

Some Books for Further Reading

These books are arranged in chronological order of publication.

An Encyclopaedia of Cottage, Farm and Villa Architecture. J. C. Loudon, 1833
  (This book is a mine of contemporary information which, despite its title, also deals
  with furniture of the period. A new edition was published in 1857.)
The Evolution of the English House. S. O. Addy, 1933
Architecture in Britain, 1530 to 1830. J. Summerson, 1953
English Furniture Styles, from 1500 to 1830. R. Fastnedge, 1964 (Pelican Books)
World Furniture. Ed. H. Hayward, 1965
Victorian Architecture. R. F. Jordan, 1966 (Pelican Books)
The Country Life Pocket Guide to English Domestic Architecture. A. L. Osborne, 1967
The Victorian Country House. M. Girouard, 1971
The English Home. H. Priestly, 1971
English Furniture: an illustrated handbook. M. Tomlin, 1972
The Georgians at Home. E. Jenkins, 1973 (Arrow Books)
Chippendale and all the rest: some influences on eighteenth-century English furniture. L. Hewitt,
  1974
The Early Victorians at Home. E. Jenkins, 1974 (Arrow Books)
The English Country House: an art and a way of life. O. Cooke, 1974
English Decoration in the 18th century. J. Fowler and J. Cornforth, 1974
The Making of the English Country House. M. Airs, 1975

Inexpensive facsimiles of the pattern books of Chippendale, Hepplewhite and Sheraton
have been produced by Dover Publications of New York, and are generally available
from most good bookshops.

The diaries of Samuel Pepys and of John Evelyn are seemingly inexhaustible sources
of valuable information about the post-1660 period, and both are available in several
different editions. However, Pepys is definitely the more readable, and most people
who are not looking for a specific reference will probably be content with the concise but
delightful Everybody's edition with illustrations by E. H. Shepard, first published in
1926.

Finally, nobody who has the interests of the country house at heart should fail to
read *The Destruction of the Country House, 1875–1975,* a collection of depressing but

thought-provoking essays by a number of experts, published in connection with an exhibition of the same title that was held in 1975 at the Victoria and Albert Museum. The book shows clearly just how much has been lost and, what is more important, how much will go in the very near future, unless both Government and people together evolve a responsible and constructive attitude towards this priceless aspect of our national heritage.

Index